This Is My Body,
This Is My Blood

Miracles of the Eucharist

Bob and Penny Lord

Journeys of Faith
1-800-633-2484

Books by Bob and Penny Lord

This Is My Body, This Is My Blood
Miracles of the Eucharist - Book I
This Is My Body, This Is My Blood
Miracles of the Eucharist - Book II
The Many Faces of Mary Book I - a Love Story
The Many Faces of Mary - Book II
Saints and Other Powerful Women in the Church
Saints and Other Powerful Men in the Church
Heavenly Army of Angels
Scandal of the Cross and Its Triumph
Martyrs - They Died for Christ
The Rosary - The Life of Jesus and Mary
Visionaries, Mystics and Stigmatists
Visions of Heaven, Hell and Purgatory
Trilogy Book I - Treasures of the Church
Trilogy Book II - Tragedy of the Reformation
Trilogy Book III - Cults, Battle of the Angels
Super Saints Book I - Journey to Sainthood
Super Saints Book II - Holy Innocence
Super Saints Book III - Defenders of the Faith
Beyond Sodom and Gomorrah
The Journey and the Dream
Miracles of the Cross
Miracles of the Child Jesus
Saints - Maligned, Misunderstood and Mistreated
Este es Mi Cuerpo - Esta es Mi Sangre
Milagros de la Eucaristía

Los Muchos Rostros de Maria - Una historia de Amor

28th Printing - 2011

ISBN 978-0-926143-02-9
Cover Art by Denys de Solére

Dedication

This dedication could be a book in itself. There are so many people who have felt the importance of getting the message of the Eucharistic Miracles to the people. There is more of an urgency today than ever before for our Church community to know and adore Jesus in this ongoing miracle. The Lord gathered up His people from all over the world to take part in this undertaking. Let us say at the outset that there is no way that we could have done this book by ourselves. We've researched these shrines for eleven years, but without a string of God's workers from as far away as Siena, Italy to Baton Rouge, Louisiana to Redlands, California, it could not have happened. We use words like Encouragement, Support, Enthusiasm when what we really mean is life's blood, taking from the heart, suffering, doing without. It goes on and on.

There has been an extraordinary amount of love and selflessness poured out by all the people who have helped us from the very beginning of this endeavor. St. Paul talks about the Body of Christ. All the members have different jobs, but without each of these, the Body can't function. Our little band was and is that Body of Christ. No matter what we say here, we can't begin to adequately thank these people for making it into the reality you're about to read. But here we go.

Our family—The family always does the most amount of suffering, and gets the least amount of attention. They have had to go through the labor pains and birth of this Child with us, and now that the baby's born, the book is finished, they will stand off on the sidelines in the shadows, while we take the accolades.

Sr. Clare Lord, Our Daughter—has forced us to go beyond ourselves, not to become comfortable in what we had, but to search out more. She was our source of encouragement when it seemed like our whole world was falling down on top of us. But when things got rough, she was able to sneak away to the peace and quiet of her Abused Wives and Children's Shelter in San Bernardino.

Rob Ziminsky, Our Grandson—on the other hand, had nowhere to go. He not only lives with us, but he works for us. Rob began his first Journey of Faith when he was ten. Rob forced us to look up at the beautiful murals of the Lord and His Mother, rather than down to the messes in the streets. Seeing Our Lord through Rob's eyes, growing with him, witnessing the faith of a child and now his wisdom as a fine young man, has brought us through many rough times in our lives. He has had to correct, and re-correct, and make so many changes in the manuscript, that he knows the words of this book by heart. A self-styled theologian at 19 years old, he is a glutton for punishment. When he disagreed with some of our writings, we got into hot and heavy discussions as to who was right and who was wrong.

Ted & Beverly Miller, Baton Rouge, Louisiana—We have never met such a committed, selfless, positive couple in our lives. The phone bills from Louisiana to California have been astronomical. This dear couple, who have been suffering their own brand of hell during the writing of this book, have been supportive in a way that is unheard of in our society. Without going into great detail, let it suffice to say that this work, this book would never have seen the light of day without their support.

John & Annabel Joyce, Mission Hills, California—Annabel

has been a supporter of ours since 1976, when we wanted to start up our first Legion of Mary Presidium. When we began our Journeys of Faith ministry, Annabel was the first to help us. When we told her of our plans for this book on the Eucharistic Miracles, she and John made the grueling trip out to our offices every day to help in research, compiling and correcting.

Luz Elena Sandoval, Oxnard, California—Every office has to have that one person that wears 9 or 10 hats. In our Ministry, that person is Luz Elena. She does everything, and trains everybody. She is our office manager. She pays all the bills. She writes all the airline tickets for each group. She takes groups out on Pilgrimage. She is in charge of our Spanish Ministry, which gets bigger and bigger every year. We pray that she will translate this book into Spanish, so that we may make it available to this most important group within our Church. We're only afraid she'll have to do this in her sleep.

Valerie Smith, Redlands, California—Valerie has been given the gift of tongues. She has taken on the horrendous task of translating information which we could only get in Italian or French, and putting it into English for us. While the authors were locked up in a room in Thousand Oaks, only allowed to come out to eat every now and then, Valerie was imprisoned in Redlands, forced by the Holy Spirit to continue until she was finished.

Fr. Antonio Giannini, Siena, Italy—Fr. Giannini is the custodian of the Eucharistic Miracle of Siena. We met him in 1981, when we first discovered this miracle. Over the years, he has given us valuable information on the various Eucharistic Miracles in Europe. Every time we went back to Siena, two or three times a year, he had new information on shrines for us to research. After our first meeting in 1981, Fr. Giannini predicted that we would write a book on the Eucharistic Miracles. Five years later, his prediction has come true.

Fr. Lewis della Zizza, Lanciano, Italy—Fr. Zizza is the superior of the Church of the Eucharistic Miracle in Lanciano. He has helped us from the first day we met him at the shrine. He also explains the shrine to our pilgrims when we bring them to Lanciano. A great deal of our inspiration and love for the gift of the Eucharistic Miracle at Lanciano came from long discussions with this learned priest.

Monsignor Don Giacomo Puri, Bolsena, Italy—Msgr. Puri is the custodian of this most important shrine of the Eucharistic Miracle of Bolsena. He doesn't usually work with pilgrims, but the good Monsignor was kind enough to take us through the shrine, spending hours explaining the background of the church as it relates to the miracle, and also in relation to the early Church, and St. Christina. He has written a brief guide to the Basilica in four languages.

Dr. Jeffrey Mirus, Trinity Communications—A selfless man, Dr. Mirus saw the need for *Journeys of Faith* to publish this book, and made it possible. In addition to gently and kindly editing our manuscript, he set the type, laid it out, and designed the cover. All that the Lord had taught him in his life was poured into this work of love.

Jim and Patti Cunningham, Gadsen, Alabama—A young couple of faith, Jim and Patti have turned their lives over to the Lord. They have such faith in the message of this book, and our Ministry that Jim has come to New Orleans with us to give talks, to California to help us with our Congress, all at his own expense. His dear family support us by doing without Jim during his absences. They have also dug down deep and given us financial help, without which we could not have done our third printing.

We know there are people we've left out. We apologize for not honoring you by name, but we thank you with all our heart for all of your tireless efforts to help the Lord through us. You are the saints we honor on All Saints Day, unnamed, but by no means forgotten. We love you.

Table of Contents

Rome, 1979: Pope John Paul II carries the Eucharist in a Corpus Christi procession.

Introduction

During the Holy Mass recently, a priest raised the host in consecration, and said the following words, *"This is My Body, I think."* Then he raised the chalice, and said *"This is My Blood, I think."*

In another instance, a priest said "Until we get rid of the Hocus Pocus in our Faith, we'll never get the people back. The idea that Christ physically comes down to us in bread and wine is ridiculous."

During a convert class this year, when the subject was going to be *The Body of Christ,* a couple asked if they could share slides on the Eucharistic Miracles. The reply was, *"That's not the Body of Christ. We the people are the Body of Christ."*

In a CCD Confirmation Class a few years ago, when some Catechists were reviewing the Sacrament of the Eucharist, they seemed to hit a stone wall. Finally, the catechists asked the crucial question, "You do believe in the physical presence of Jesus in the Eucharist?!" The kindest response of the children was, "How many millions of Jesus' can there be?" It went downhill to "You expect me to believe that because some man puts his hands over bread and wine, and says some words, that Jesus comes down into them?"

This cut like a knife into the Catechists because some of these young people shaking their heads negatively, sorrow in some of their eyes, had been prepared by the same Catechists for First Holy Communion 6 years before. When the instructors brought the problem to the priest's attention, and asked that the children not be allowed to be confirmed if they could not honestly accept Jesus' presence in the Eucharist, his answer was, "Well, today, we're trying to show people how Jesus is present in other ways than the Eucharist, in the Word, in the . . ." The teacher cut him off, and added "in the trees, in the air, at the beach, in bed at home. If that's so, Father, what do we need you for?"

The above statements and situations may seem shocking, and indeed they are. But they are not new. Controversy over the physical presence of Christ in the Eucharist, that He truly gives us His Body and Blood in the form of bread and wine, has been with us since the beginning of Christ's ministry.

In John 6:51, while Jesus was teaching the Jews at the synagogue in Capharnaum, He gave us the first Eucharistic Doctrine. He called Himself "The Bread of Life".

" '*I myself am the living bread come down from heaven. If anyone eats this bread, he shall live forever; the bread I will give is my flesh, for the life of the world.'*

At this the Jews quarreled among themselves, saying, 'How can he give us his flesh to eat?' Thereupon Jesus said to them: 'Let me solemnly assure you, if you do not eat the flesh of the Son of Man and drink his blood, you have no life in you.' "

After saying this, He lost most of His followers. They couldn't live with this statement. Jesus, God-Man, had to have known what would happen. In His humaness, He knew what He should do. But He knew what He had to do. It would have been so much easier for Him to call them all back, and say "Wait a minute. I wasn't serious. I was just testing you." But He was serious. He couldn't compromise the truth. He knew the tremendous task He had to accomplish, and the short time available to get it done. If this controversial statement were not true, as so many would have us believe, why did He risk all that

He had accomplished? Why was He not willing to back down from it? Even after they questioned Him on it, saying, "This sort of talk is hard to endure. How can anyone take it seriously?", His comment was, *"Does it shake your faith?"*

Jesus was so firm on this point that He was even willing to lose the Apostles. This was the moment of decision for them. He asked the twelve apostles, *"Will you leave me also?"* Peter said, "Where are we to go ? You have the words of everlasting life."

The Eucharistic Doctrine was repeated innumerable times by the three Synoptic Gospel writers, as well as by St. John, and St. Paul. It was stressed more than any teaching in Christ's ministry. If Jesus was so adamant about this principle, how do we dare speculate on what He really meant?

Bishop Fulton J. Sheen, a 20th Century Prophet and staunch defender of the Eucharist, tells us that when Jesus made the first Eucharistic statement, Judas began his plot to betray the Lord. He couldn't accept the doctrine of the Eucharist.

We have a tendency to make severe judgments on those we consider "weak sisters", disciples who walked away from Jesus when He made the Eucharistic statement. It should be easier for us. We've had two thousand years of tradition in this belief. We've grown up with it. It's become almost rote to us. We don't consider what might have gone through the minds of His disciples at that time. We have to consider *who* these people were. They were Jews. They lived by Mosaic Law. They were not allowed to drink animal blood, much less human blood. Taken literally, this Nazarean was talking about cannibalism. There were religious cannibal cults in the hills of Israel at the time. They just didn't understand what Jesus truly meant, and so they left.

From Capharnaum to the Cenacle, the cycle is completed. On Holy Thursday evening, in the Upper Room at the Last Supper, we were given the gift, the everlasting gift of the Flesh and Blood of Jesus. In Luke 22:19, we read:

"Then taking bread and giving thanks, He broke it and

The site of the Upper Room where Jesus instituted the Eucharist on Holy Thursday (top), and the Synagogue in Capharnaum where He made His first Eucharistic statement (Jn 6:51).

gave it to them, saying: *'This is My Body to be given for you. Do this as a remembrance of Me.'* He did the same with the cup after eating, saying as He did so: *'This Cup is the New Covenant in My Blood, which will be shed for you.'* " It was after this that Judas left the room to complete his plan for betrayal.

We Catholics are accused of being non-biblical, and yet this Biblical statement by Jesus, which is the backbone of our Faith, is rejected by Protestants, even Fundamentalist Baptists, who claim "If it's not in the Bible, I don't believe in it." But this is Scriptural. This is in the Bible. Why won't you believe in it?

The Eucharist is the most important truth of our faith. This is what separates us from our brothers and sisters in Christ of the Protestant denominations. We believe in the everlasting gift of the Body and Blood of Christ in the Eucharist, brought to us each day in miracle form on every altar in the world, at the Consecration of the Mass, Just as Jesus commanded. History is filled with the tales of brave men and women who gave up *their* body and blood in defense and protection of the Body and Blood of Jesus.

Heresies began cropping up as early as the end of the first century, regarding the physical presence of Christ in the Eucharist. St. Ignatius of Antioch, one of the first defenders of the Eucharist, as he was being taken to Rome to be devoured by the lions, wrote letters to St. Polycarp regarding the errors of the heretics concerning the physical presence of Jesus in the Eucharist.

Questions of every sort were raised throughout the centuries. Does the bread and wine actually become the Body and Blood of Christ? Is the Host a symbol rather than Jesus Himself? Can a priest, whom we know is a sinner, change bread and wine into the Body and Blood of Christ? How worthy must a man be before he can achieve this miracle?

Bishop Sheen tells us that priests go bad when they lose their faith in the Eucharist. "They may tell you," he says, "that they can't live without a woman, or that they can't take the rigidity of the priesthood, or that the religious life is just not for them, but what has happened is that they've lost their faith in the Eucharist." Bishop Sheen spent an hour before the Blessed Sacrament each day of his priesthood. When he prepared his very successful TV Show, Life is Worth Living, he discussed his script ideas with Our Lord in the Blessed Sacrament before he would finalize each program.

On the other side of the coin, pagans in early Christian days unwittingly performed a Eucharistic ceremony. In Siracusa Sicily, they brought the dying to the amphitheater, as the Christians were being killed. They believed that if they ate the heart of a Christian, and drank his blood, they would be healed of an incurable disease; they wouldn't die. Don't we believe in the same thing? Even then, these pagans, without knowledge of the Eucharist, instinctively knew of the power of Christ's Body and Blood. They had the freedom to accept it. In the Eucharistic Miracle of Lanciano, in which the host turned to flesh, *a human heart,* and the wine turned into blood, *human blood,* we have a perfect parallel to this pagan custom of early Christian days. We are Catholics. We were given the gift of knowledge of this great mystery of Faith. And yet we're having a problem believing in His very own words. When St. John quotes the words of Jesus in John 6, he doesn't use the regular word for "eat". He uses the words "gnaw" or "munch" to bring across the reality of what he tells us (*New American Bible,* footnote on John 6:54-58).

Our Lord Jesus never leaves us. He is always here to help us. We feel His strength and power most especially at times of stress and doubt. His love for us is so strong that He defies the laws of nature, as a special gift to us when we begin to weaken or fall into the quicksand of doubt and anxiety, with a miracle.

The Lord gave us a mandate in 1977 to tell the world about His goodness, His kindness, His love for us, as shown to us in the various Eucharistic Miracles throughout the centuries. We first heard about the Eucharistic Miracle of Lanciano in 1976, when we went on our first Pilgrimage. But we were not able to get to visit there. The next year, we went to Lanciano, but it was during the dreaded lunch hour, from 12:00 Noon to 3:30. We arrived at about 1 pm, and didn't want to wait. Can you imagine? The following year, 1978, we arrived at Lanciano at 3 pm, and waited, pestering the local priest the entire time to open the Church.

The experience was so incredible, we could not believe our eyes. Our daughter, a Franciscan sister from San Bernardino, fell to her knees in awe. From that time on, we began bringing slides of the Eucharistic Miracles back to share with our friends in California.

We searched the European Continent for Eucharistic Miracles. We stumbled onto most of them by accident, until, because of our Franciscan daughter, we visited the Basilica of St. Francis in Siena in 1981. We had been to Siena many times, but only to learn about St. Catherine. Being a loyal Franciscan, Sister Clare insisted we visit the Church of St. Francis in the town. It was there that we saw a photo of our Pope John Paul II venerating a Eucharistic Miracle in Siena in September of 1980. The priest in the photo with His Holiness was a Fr. Antonio Giannini, custodian of the Incorrupt Hosts of Siena.

Fr. Giannini has been custodian of the Miracle of Siena for many years. He has devoted most of his life to this miracle and to study of the various Eucharistic Miracles throughout the world. His goal in life is to spread devotion to the Eucharist through the miracles the Lord has given us. We spent much time with him. He told us of all the places we should visit where there have been Eucharistic Miracles. He made a prediction when we left him that Spring day in 1981. He said "Send me a copy of the book when it's finished." We had not planned a book at that time. The purpose of our research was to bring the good news of the Eucharistic Miracles back to our Church in the United States.

We have visited most of the shrines we write about in this book. We have spoken to the priests at the shrines, taken pictures and videos where possible. We've noted all documentation that was made by local bishops over the years, as well as Papal Bulls in support of them. Also, something just as important, we've spoken to the local people. They inject their own beliefs, as well as "Storia" (History) passed down about miracles that have occurred, as a result of prayer to Our Lord Jesus present in these Eucharistic Miracles.

We began bringing Pilgrims to the Holy Places in 1980. Lanciano, Bolsena and Orvieto, Cascia and Siena have been included in every Pilgrimage to Italy. Whenever we go to Fatima, we venerate the Eucharistic Miracle at the shrine of Santarem. We started publishing a Newsletter in 1983, telling our Pilgrims about the shrines. In the first issue, we wrote about the Eucharistic Miracle of Lanciano. In June of 1984, we were interviewed on KIHS, Channel 46, a Los Angeles based Catholic Television Station. The first of the three segments we televised for them was about the Eucharistic Miracle of Lanciano. The greatest comment we received was "If only you would write a book on these miracles. It would be so good to have them all under one cover." And so, we planned the book.

However, being typical human beings, we've stalled, put it on the back burner. Many excuses came up. We don't have enough research. We have to visit more of the shrines. We're too busy. Well, the time for excuses is long past. There is an urgency we feel right now. There is no time. Too many things are happening in the world to let us think we have forever. Jesus is gathering up His children. He wants all of us. Like the Good Shepherd that He is, He's using every tool and weapon He can find including unworthy servants, like us, to return to Him His lost sheep.

We've grouped these special occurrences under a heading *Eucharistic Miracles*. These are miracles of the Eucharist that were given to us by Our Lord, witnessed and documented by the Church. Because the Eucharist is so important, and because these signs were needed so badly either to strengthen the faith of an individual or a group within the church, or the whole Church, the Lord allowed these manifestations to occur at various times and in various places throughout history.

We believe in these miracles. We've been to these shrines and witnessed these gifts from the Lord. We have seen with our own eyes, stood inches away from Our Lord, His arms outstretched, speaking to us. "Here I am. Here is my very Heart. All you have to do is Take Me, I'm Yours." The Church doesn't require anyone to believe in these miracles. But it also doesn't require that we not believe. After having viewed these miracles, and read the background on them, our constant reply is "why not"? Our personal attitude is just the reverse of the attitude in "Why do bad things happen to good people?", where the author presents God as helpless to prevent bad things from happening. To us that's putting God into a box, limiting what He can do. We don't believe anything is beyond God.

Franz Werfel, a Jewish convert to Catholicism and author of The Song of Bernadette, said about our Lady's apparitions to Bernadette Soubirous in Lourdes, France, in 1858, "For those who believe, no explanation is necessary. For those who do not believe, no explanation is possible."

We believe the same can be said of the Physical Presence of Our Lord Jesus in the Eucharist. Jesus tells us in John 29:21, Blessed are those who have not seen, and still believe. But He knows us as well as He knew Thomas. He knows our human failings, our weaknesses. We believe this is why He comes to us at our darkest hours, with a gift, nourishment, Grace.

If He gives us the right words, as we pray for before we begin each narrative, if He fills us with His Holy Spirit, and what we write here brings ONE lost sheep back into the fold, or prevents ONE weak sheep from leaving, we've accomplished our goal. If by researching all these shrines, visiting them, speaking to the priests there, translating the information they give us, writing these things down, getting them out to you, if all these things help us with our own faith, we can be joyful, feeling that we've done our job.

We pray that the Lord give us the right words, right for you. We pray that ONLY THE RIGHT WORDS reach your consciousness, and those that are not of Him bounce off you like raindrops. We pray that He empties us of all that is us, and fills us with all that is Him, and that all of this comes to you.

On Sunday, June 17, 1979, the Feast of Corpus Christi, Pope John Paul II gave his Sunday talk and blessing to the Faithful from his apartment window at St. Peter's Square in Rome. He said to us:

"This evening, at St. John Lateran's, I will celebrate a solemn Mass in honor of the Feast of the Body and Blood of Our Lord Jesus. This will be followed by a procession of the Eucharist from the Church of St. John Lateran to the Church of St. Mary Major. Do not let Jesus walk alone."

The Secular Press, in protest of the traffic jam that was created that night, estimated that over 200,000 people attended the outdoor Mass at St. John Lateran, and processed to St. Mary Major with Jesus and our beloved Pope.

We invite you to walk with Jesus through the Eucharistic Miracles in this book. He has again become completely vulnerable in order to give us the strength we need to believe. We say, as our Pope before us has said, "Don't let Jesus walk alone."

Lanciano, 700's A.D.:
The Heart of Christ

Lanciano is a small, medieval town, nestled in from the coast of the Adriatic Sea in Italy, halfway between San Giovanni Rotondo and Loreto. Everything about Lanciano smacks of the Eucharistic Miracle. Even the name of the town was changed from Anxanum (in ancient times) to Lanciano, meaning "The Lance". Tradition has it that the centurion Longinus, who thrust the Lance into the side of Jesus, striking Him in the Tip of His Heart from which He shed blood and water, (in the Gospel account of the Crucifixion (Mk 15:29)) was from this town. After seeing the events which followed the piercing of Jesus' heart, the darkening of the sun, and the earthquake, he believed that Christ was the Savior. A more physical sign, however, was that Longinus had had poor eyesight, and after having touched his eyes with the water and blood from the side of Jesus, his eyesight was restored. What a perfect parallel the actions of the Centurion were to the Eucharistic Miracle. He touched the Heart of Jesus, was healed, and converted. He gave up the Army, went to Cappadocia, and was martyred for the faith. He is known now as Saint Longinus. His feast day is celebrated on March 15.

The church of the Eucharistic Miracle is located in the center of the town. But what is the center of the town today was the outskirts of the town back in the Eighth Century, when the Eucharistic Miracle occurred. At the time, it was called the Church of St. Legontian and St. Domitian, and was under the custody of the Basilian Monks of the Greek Orthodox Rite. This was prior to the Great Schism of 1054.

A Basilian monk, wise in the ways of the world, but not in the ways of faith, was having a trying time with his belief in the real presence of Our Lord Jesus in the Eucharist. He prayed constantly for relief from his doubts, and from the fear that he was losing his vocation. He suffered through the routine of his priesthood day after day, with these doubts gnawing at him.

The situation in the world did not help strengthen his faith. There were many heresies cropping up all the time, which kept chipping away at his faith. They were not all from outside the church either. Brother priests and bishops were victims of these heresies, and they were being spread throughout the church. This priest couldn't seem to help being more and more convinced by the logic of these heresies, especially the one concerning his particular problem, the physical presence of Jesus in the Eucharist.

One morning, while he was having a strong attack of doubt, he began the Consecration of the Mass for the people of the town. He used the same size host which is used in the Latin Rite masses today. What he beheld as he consecrated the bread and wine caused his hands to shake, indeed his whole body. He stood for a long time with his back to the people, and then slowly turned around to them.

He said: "O fortunate witnesses to whom the Blessed God, to confound my disbelief, has wished to reveal Himself in this Most Blessed Sacrament and to render Himself visible to our eyes. Come, brethren, and marvel at our God so close to us. Behold the Flesh and Blood of our most beloved Christ."

The host had turned into Flesh. The wine had turned into Blood.

The people, having witnessed the miracle for themselves, began to wail, asking for forgiveness, crying for mercy. Others began beating their breasts, confessing their sins, declaring themselves unworthy to witness such a miracle. Still others went down on their knees in respect, and thanksgiving for the gift the Lord had bestowed on them. All spread the story throughout the town and surrounding villages.

Jesus even allowed Himself to be crucified again. After the miracle, the Host was pinned down to a wooden board, so that when it dried, it would not curl up, as scabbed flesh does. So here He was again, with nails in His Body, nailed to a piece of wood.

The miracle that occurred in 700 was just the beginning. That was 1250 years ago. Had that miracle taken place, and then the flesh and blood disintegrated, as would have been normal, the miracle would have been none the less a miracle. The priest's faith had been renewed. The entire town, the whole country for that matter, became aware of the miracle. Pilgrims flocked to Lanciano to venerate the Host turned flesh. Belief in the Eucharist had been reborn. The gift from the Lord was complete.

But that's not all. The miracle is ongoing. The Host-turned-Flesh, and the wine-turned-Blood, without the use of any form of preservative, is still present in the reliquary. In 1574 testing was done on the Flesh and Blood and an unexplainable phenomenon was discovered. The five pellets of coagulated Blood are different sizes and shapes. But any combination weighs the same as the total. In other words, 1 weighs the same as 2, 2 weigh the same as 3, and 3 weigh the same as 5.

From the very beginning, the local church accepted this miracle as a true sign from heaven, and venerated the Eucharistic Flesh and Blood in processions on its feast day, the last Sunday of October. The fame of the shrine spread throughout the region quickly, and soon all of Italy came to the Church in Pilgrimage.

Many accounts authenticating the Eucharistic Miracle have been written over the years. Because this has been such an important local miracle, the background and history of the events were carefully recorded.

There had been a manuscript written in both Greek and Latin, attesting to the miracle. It was said to have been written and certified at the time of the miracle. In a Chronology of the City of Lanciano, historian Fella wrote that in early 1500 two Basilian Monks came to the Church, which was now in the custody of the Franciscans, and asked to stay overnight. They also asked to see the parchment which told the story of the Eucharistic Miracle of Lanciano. The Franciscans allowed them to study the parchment overnight. But the next morning, the Basilian Monks left very early, before the Franciscans had awakened, and took the manuscripts with them. The motive, it was thought, was that the Basilian Monks were ashamed that one of their own had lost his faith in the Eucharist, and hoped that by stealing the original document attesting to the event, it might go away. The Church of the miracle remained in the custody of the Monks of St. Basil, until 1176, when the Benedictines took over. However, the building had become very run down, and the Benedictines were not overly excited about taking care of it. The Franciscans, however, did want custodianship of the Shrine. When one of their benefactors, Bishop Landulfo, was made Bishop of Chieti, he gave them the Shrine to take care of. So, in 1252, the Benedictines left, and the Franciscans took over. What they were not aware of until they actually came to Lanciano was that the church was a disaster. They surmised that this was why the Benedictines so easily turned it over to them. In 1258, the Franciscans built a new church on the site of the original Church of St. Legontian.

In 1515, Pope Leo X made Lanciano an episcopal See, directly responsible to Rome.   In 1562, Pope Pius IV wrote a Papal Bull raising it to an Archepiscopal See.

In 1666, the Franciscans found themselves in the middle of

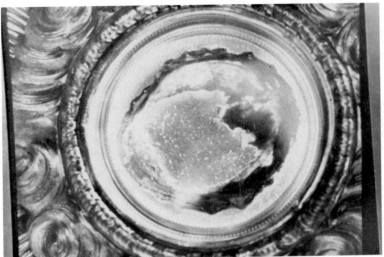

At Lanciano: It is believed that this chalice was used on the day of the Miracle; it contains the Blood. The Flesh is from a real human heart (bottom).

a legal battle with what was called the "Raccomandati", or Select group of the town. Today's Italians might call them "I Superbi". They thought they were better than everyone else. The Raccomandati tried to take the church away from the Franciscans by laying claim to the original church of St. Legontian, upon which the Franciscan church was built. If they had won, they would have had both churches. But the Lord intervened through the high ranking Cardinal Giannetti, of the Sacred Congregation of Bishops and Religious, and the Franciscans won the case. You can be sure that they immediately applied for a deed, and 18 years later, in 1684, it was granted them. During Napoleon's time, in 1809, the Franciscans were driven out of the town. But they returned in solemn triumph on June 21, 1953.

On June 25, 1672, Pope Clement X declared the altar of the Eucharistic Miracle a privileged altar on the Octave day of the deceased and on all Mondays of the year. In 1887, the Archbishop of Lanciano, Monsignore Petarca, obtained from Pope Leo XIII, a plenary indulgence in perpetuity to those who venerate the Eucharistic Miracle during the 8 days preceding the feast day.

The Eucharistic Miracle was placed in different locations within the Church of St. Francis over the years. At one point, in 1566, the threat of the Turks became imminent along the Adriatic Coast. It was thought that Lanciano would be an easy target for them. As a matter of security, the Eucharistic Miracle was taken from its chapel and walled up on the other side of the Church. It got to a point, however, that the threat of the Turks became too much of a reality. On August 1 of that year, a Friar Giovanni Antonio di Mastro Renzo lost his faith, not in the Eucharist, but either in God's ability or God's desire to save him and his little band of Franciscans from the onslaught of the Turks. Using the need to save the Eucharistic Miracle from the Infidels, he took the reliquary containing the Flesh and Blood, and with his Friars fled the city. They walked all through the night. Just before dawn, Friar Giovanni felt they had put enough distance between them and the enemy, and ordered his friars to rest. As the sun came up, they found that they were back at the gates of the city.

Believing that the Lord had intervened, and that He wanted His Sacred Sign as an assurance to the people of the city of Lanciano that He had not abandoned them, the friars were filled with the Holy Spirit. They acquired the courage of lions. They vowed to remain in the Church, and protect the Eucharistic Miracle with their lives. As it turned out, the Lord kept them from harm, as well as the city of Lanciano, and the Eucharistic Miracle.

The Flesh and Blood were kept walled up until 1636, although the threat of the invading Turks had long since disappeared. At that time, the Eucharistic Miracle was transferred to the right side of the altar, encased in an iron tabernacle, behind iron doors. There were four keys to the vault, each held by different people in the town. This was called the Valsecca Chapel, in honor of the benefactor. The Miraculous Flesh and Blood were kept in this chapel until 1902. The faithful were only able to venerate the Eucharistic Miracle on special occasions, the Monday after Easter, and the last week in October, the week of the feast. The Plenary Indulgence was available to the people during the feast.

By 1902, it was determined that the Valsecca Chapel was inadequate for the Eucharistic Miracle. The people of Lanciano were hungry to be able to see Our Lord Jesus in the form of Flesh and Blood while they prayed to Him. Under the inspiration of the local bishop of Lanciano, Bishop Petrarca, a beautiful altar and new home for the Eucharistic Miracle was designed by a well known architect, Filippo Sergiacomo. That was a beautiful sign. But the real sign came from the people of Lanciano. They collected all the money needed for the new altar. During the month of the feast, five bishops from the Abruzzi region, with the Franciscans, and pilgrims from all over, solemnly dedicated the new altar.

Lanciano was selected as the site for the First Eucharistic Congress for the region of Abruzzi on September 23-25, 1921.

We bring our pilgrims to this shrine many times each year. Upon entering the church, our attention is immediately focused on the unusual altar. There are two tabernacles, rather than the traditional one. The second tabernacle is on top of the first. Continuing down the aisle toward the main altar, we see a large tablet on the wall, dating back to 1574, which tells the story of the Eucharistic Miracle.

Further on the right of the main altar is a painting of the Eucharistic Miracle. The painting opens out from the wall, revealing a set of doors, behind which is hidden an old iron tabernacle. This is the Valsecca Chapel, and was the home of the Eucharistic Miracle from 1636 until 1902, when the present altar was built.

We walk to the back of the main altar, where there is a stairway leading up to the second tabernacle, to the Eucharistic Miracle. A priest from the church dresses in vestments worn for the celebration of Holy Mass, and leads us to the top of the stairway. The Monstrance and the miracle are before our eyes. We are allowed to ascend in groups of five. The priest puts a flashlight in back of the Host turned Flesh. This is an actual heart muscle. With the light in the background, the fibers of the heart can be seen. The chalice which holds the Blood is believed to be the same one into which the Blood was placed after the miracle, and possibly the actual chalice which was used for the Mass when the miracle took place. The Host has turned light brown over the years. When the priest puts the light in back of It, It appears rose colored. The Blood has an ochre appearance.

It's impossible to truly appreciate the Eucharistic Miracle of Lanciano without seeing the impact it has on those who witness it.

All questions and doubts about the physical presence of Jesus in the Eucharist become a matter of rhetoric when you are privileged to witness those who have seen the miracle. They descend the steps in tears. Many go down on their knees at the

The two tabernacles at Lanciano: the top one contains the Eucharistic Miracle.

sight of the miracle. What had possibly been curious, doubting Thomases become dumbfounded, awestruck believers. They go back to their pews and just sit there, silent, weeping, praying. One priest who went with us to Lanciano in 1983 wrote to us, "I can never raise the host or wine in Consecration again, without seeing my Lord's very Heart between my fingers, His Blood alive in the Chalice before me."

A pilgrim, born and baptised Catholic, shared with his convert wife, after venerating the Eucharistic Miracle of Lanciano, "I never believed in the physical presence of Jesus in the Eucharist. To me, it was strictly 'in memory of Him'. Now, I truly believe that my Jesus comes alive to me personally in the Consecrated Host that I consume at Holy Mass."

On one occasion, after the priest had shown all our pilgrims the Eucharistic Miracle, he came down to the foot of the altar, and made the following observation:

"Remember, this miracle that you are witnessing now, and that you have traveled so far to witness, happens every day in every church in the world, at the consecration of the Mass."

How many tests have been made over the years, how many times Our Dear Lord Jesus allows Himself to be prodded and cut, examined under microscopes, and photographed. The most recent, an extensive scientific research done in 1970, used the most modern scientific tools available. The results of the tests are as follows:

- The flesh is real flesh. The blood is real blood.
- The flesh consists of the muscular tissue of the heart (myocardium)
- The flesh and blood belong to the human species.
- The flesh and blood have the same blood type (AB).
- In the blood, there were found proteins in the same normal proportions as are found in the sero-proteic make up of fresh, normal blood.
- In the blood, there were also found these minerals: Chlorides,

phosphorous, magnesium, potassium, sodium and calcium.
- The preservation of the flesh and of the blood, which were left in their natural state for twelve centuries (without any chemical preservatives) and exposed to the action of atmospheric and biological agents, remains an extraordinary phenomenon.

As part of this most recent investigation, the following comment was made: "Though it is alien to my task strictly speaking, I feel I should insert the following reflection into the study just completed: the clarification, which comes through in these studies, of the nature of the flesh gives little support to the hypothesis of a 'fraud' perpetrated centuries ago. As a matter of fact supposing that the heart may have been taken from a cadaver, I maintain that only a hand experienced in anatomic dissection would have been able to obtain from a hollow internal organ such a uniform cut (as can still be glimpsed in the flesh)."

What the doctor, a scientist and not a theologian, is saying in simple language is that although it's not his task to speculate, it would have been difficult, next to *impossible*, for anyone to have cut a slice of the heart in the way that it was done. He also states that it's highly doubtful that there was any fraud involved.

Another unusual characteristic of the blood is that when liquified, it has retained the chemical properties of freshly shed blood. When we cut ourselves and stain our clothes, the chemical properties of the blood are gone within 20 minutes to a half hour. If blood is not refrigerated within an hour maximum, the composition rapidly breaks down. If blood were taken from a dead body, it would lose its qualities quickly through decay. This blood is over 1250 years old and still contains all its properties, chemicals and protein of freshly shed blood. And yet in the testing, it was determined that *no preservatives of any kind* were found in the blood.

Jesus gives us His Heart again in the Eucharistic Miracle,

which is a Heart muscle. He gives us His Blood again in this miraculous form to heal us. He gives us His Blood with His Body in the Eucharist every day to heal us and nourish us. There are instances in history, which we'll explore in this book, where people lived for years on no other nourishment than the Eucharist.

"He who feeds on my flesh and drinks my blood has life eternal, and I will raise him up on the last day. For my flesh is real food, and my blood real drink." John 6:54-56

We believe that the most perfect form of love is the Eucharistic Love of Jesus. In the Miracle of Lanciano, He loves us by revealing His very Heart and His very Blood. It helps us to understand the sacrifice of our Perfect Lamb, Jesus, in the Holy Mass. *How much do I love you? Here is my Heart. How much do I love you? Here is my blood, being shed for you.*

Each day during the Mass, Jesus, completely vulnerable, offers us His very heart for us to accept or reject. We become part of the Incarnation again: God, one with man—God becoming man. As Mary carried Jesus below her heart, we too are allowed to carry now Jesus' very Heart, His Body, His Love in our heart. And we are never the same.

As a postscript to the Miracle of Lanciano, we should note that in 1978, a group of scientists from NASA performed an intensive examination on the Shroud of Turin, using all the sophisticated scientific equipment available to our Space Agency at that time. Among the many findings the scientists made in support of the authenticity of the Shroud, a very significant discovery was found regarding the blood type on the Shroud. It was AB positive, the same blood type as found in the Eucharistic Miracle of Lanciano. More and more, science has verified what we have believed in Faith for centuries.

Offida, 1273: Shedding His Blood

The Lord allows Himself to be drawn back to Lanciano again. This could very well be called the Eucharistic Miracle of Lanciano II, because what we call the Miracle of Offida actually happened in Lanciano in the year 1273.

Why did Jesus pick Lanciano yet a second time? What was the need for Him to manifest Himself again in this town in another miraculous way? To the inquisitive mind, the scientific mind, there has to be a logical explanation for a phenomenon such as this. But there is no way that we can anticipate Our Lord's actions because they defy the laws of logic. I sometimes believe He does this intentionally.

St. Thomas Aquinas, the great Doctor of the Church and one of the most brilliant minds the world has ever known, was given a revelation towards the end of his life. Afterwards, he stopped writing and dictating his great Summa Theologica. When asked why he was abandoning his work, he replied, "The end of my labors has come. All that I have written appears to be as so much straw after the things that have been revealed to me." We are thrilled about the prospect of what God will reveal to us when we meet Him in the Kingdom. But until that time, we can only try to speculate on the mysteries of God's ways. The Second Eucharistic Miracle of Lanciano, or as it is better known, the Eucharistic Miracle of Offida is one of the mysteries of God's way.

The principal characters in this miraculous account are a newlywed couple, Ricciarella and Giacomo (James) Stasio, their mule, and a witch. Apparently, the newlyweds' marriage was not made in heaven. They had nothing in common. Giacomo cared more for his mule than for his wife. There is no indication as to what was the cause of their problem, whether the wife was at fault or the husband. We do know that the wife, Ricciarella, wanted a better life for them. She thought if they had a better sex life, they would be more happily married. She never considered getting even with her husband for his treatment of her, or of having extra-marital affairs. She just wanted a better life with him.

To this end, she enlisted the services of a local sorceress, or witch. The witch had a powerful reputation for bringing the excitement back into marriages whose fire had gone out. The witch prescribed the following potion:

"Go to Communion, but don't swallow the Host. Take it home, put it in the stove, and burn it. Take the ashes, and throw them into his wine or his soup. Then let me know the effect. You'll see that he will 'walk in heat like cats on a fence'."

This description of how her husband would react to the potion gave Ricciarella just the incentive she needed to justify committing this terrible act. She knew, because of her upbringing in the faith, that this was an act of Sacrilege. We have to wonder how she must have wrestled with her conscience before she made the decision to perform this horrible act.

Whatever justification finally gave her the courage, she set out for the church to take part in the Mass, and receive Our Dear Lord Jesus in Communion. Her heart pounded as she rehearsed the plot over and over again in her mind. At the proper time, Ricciarella, looking like a little saint, went up to the priest to receive Communion. After having received the Host, she turned away from the priest quickly, so that she could remove the Lord from her mouth. She made sure she was not caught in the act.

She left the Church and ran through the streets of Lanciano until she reached her home. Her hands shook violently. She started a fire under an earthen pot. Then, when it was very hot, she took the Host, and placed It in the pot. It began to smoke. She could not take her eyes away from the wickedness she was performing. The driving force that prevented her from stopping this madness was the change she fantasized would take place in her husband towards her. The outside of the Host turned into flesh, and began to bleed profusely. The center of the Host retained its original form. The blood gushed from the Host Turned Flesh.

She panicked. She didn't know what to do. The blood covered the bottom of the pot, which was filling quickly. She took wax and dirt and threw them into the pot. She filled the pot with dirt, but the blood seeped through the dirt, rising to the top of the pot. She grabbed a huge linen table cloth and wrapped the pot in it. She didn't know where to put it. She ran out to the stable, and dug a hole in the dung of the mule. She buried the table cloth and the pot with the Eucharist inside.

When her husband returned home that evening, he noticed that the mule was acting more stubborn than usual. The animal did not want to go into the stable. Giacomo was used to a certain amount of obstinance from the mule, but this was the worst the animal had ever behaved. Giacomo tried pushing the mule, and then slapping him, all to no avail. Finally he got a whip and began beating the animal. The pain being more than the mule could endure, he reluctantly stumbled into the barn. The animal fell prostrate near where the dung was located, almost in a position of adoration.

Giacomo never needed an excuse to be unkind to Ricciarella, but if he had, the incident with the mule provided him with perfect justification. He blamed her for the behavior of the mule, accusing her of putting some spell on the stable. He gave her a few cracks with the same whip which he had used on his beast.

For Ricciarella, this was the beginning of living Hell. She felt great pangs of conscience for her sin. She came to realize more and more the seriousness and consequences of her actions. She was also beginning to wonder just how powerful the witch was, by the way her husband was treating her. The desired results of her sin never materialized. If anything, their relationship got weaker, while the feelings of guilt and remorse grew stronger by the passing day.

Ricciarella lived with this situation for *seven years*. The torture she inflicted on herself was maddening. The way that her husband continued to treat her, she believed was a punishment by God. She lost all hope. She could not accept that she could ever be forgiven by God. The pain she felt was mostly for having committed such an inexcusable crime against a God who had never hurt her. Tales of the Good God, that her mother had told her when she was a child, echoed in her mind. She yearned to confess her sin, and relieve the burden of her heart and soul. But she didn't have the courage to accept the shame she would inflict on herself, she thought, by confessing to a priest.

Finally, when she could no longer live with herself, or the self-inflicted pain she had suffered for seven years, Ricciarella contacted the prior of the local Augustinian monastery in Lanciano. This friar was a native of Offida, which will become important as our story unfolds. Ricciarella confessed her grave sin to the priest. He accompanied her back to her home. They went into the stable, and dug through the dung which had accumulated over the seven years. When the friar pulled the table cloth out, and uncovered it, he found that the contents of the pot, the bleeding Flesh and the Host, had remained incorrupt over the years.

He took the table cloth and the earthen pot containing the Host away with him. He told no one of the incident. Ricciarella was relieved because her scandal would not be spread all over the province, and her deteriorated relationship with her husband would not worsen. We're not sure what the friar's motives were. He wanted the Eucharistic Miracle taken away from Lanciano, that is known. Was it because he was sincerely afraid that if the miracle were revealed, Ricciarella would be implicated? Or did he want the glory of an incorrupt Eucharistic Miracle to be given to his home town Offida?

On a pretext, the Friar received permission from his superiors to leave the monastery. He left Lanciano in secrecy a few days later. He took the Sacred Host to a Fr. Michael Mallicani, who was the prior of the Augustinian monastery of Offida. Fr. Mallicani embraced the miracle as the property of Offida, and immediately created a sanctuary for It in that town. This was in the year 1280, seven years after Ricciarella had committed the Sacrilege.

Fr. Mallicani moved quickly. He and another friar went to Venice in the same year to have a beautiful reliquary built which was to become the home of the Eucharistic Miracle. They commissioned a goldsmith to do the work under secrecy. After he had finished the beautiful reliquary, and the priest had placed the Eucharistic Miracle inside, the friars left by boat to return to Offida. It was then that the goldsmith decided to tell the local Duke of Venice what had transpired. The Duke, anxious to get hold of a genuine Eucharistic Miracle for his own province, ordered a ship to intercept the one carrying the two friars back to Offida.

But the Lord intercepted! As the Duke's ship was about to overtake the friars, the Adriatic Sea became violent, allowing the friars to disembark at Ancona, and return safely to their monastery in Offida. The reliquary was installed in the Church in Offida. It is still there to this day.

Why was there so much intrigue and deception involved with this miracle? The Miraculous Host, which was given to us in Lanciano, was stolen by a member of the clergy, and brought to Offida, in another province.The friars in Offida were accomplices to the larcenous deed. They compounded it by going to Venice to have a reliquary made. This would, in their eyes, and the eyes of the city, validate the authority of Offida to keep the stolen Sacred Host. Why was it so important to the people involved that they would go through all that they did?

We can give light to part of the reasoning. In those days, and even today, for a town to have the reputation of having a famous saint buried there, or even better, a Eucharistic Miracle, as in this case, was for that town to become famous. People flocked from miles around to come and venerate the miracle. Whether they were pilgrims or curiosity seekers was not important to the town. What was important was that people came and spent money in their town.

Venice, scandalously involved in this miracle, boasts that the faithful can venerate the incorrupt body of St. Lucy of Siracusa, Sicily in one of their churches. There is even a big sign outside the church, facing the Grand Canal, attesting to the fact. The people from Siracusa blame the Venetians for stealing the body of the saint from their town centuries ago. On a Saturday evening in November of 1981, just hours after we had visited the Church of St. Lucy, thieves broke in and stole the body. There had been an expensive silver face mask covering St. Lucy's face, which was not taken. So robbery was ruled out. It was believed that Siracusans were responsible for the crime. St. Lucy's body has since been returned to the Church in Venice.

But in the case of Lanciano, why did the Lord allow the theft to happen? Is it possible that all these people were doing the Lord's will without realizing it? We have to go back to the very beginning of this story. The more we study the workings of the Lord, the Scripture passage "the Lord works in mysterious ways, His wonders to behold" becomes increasingly apparent. We'll have to wait until the end of the story, when we meet Him in Heaven, to find out what He was doing.

Bolsena and Orvieto, 1263: Corpus Christi

In looking back over our Church History, we can compare Jesus to an artist who blends all the proper colors, supplying muted tones and pastels to create a masterpiece of balance. Or He is like a stage director whose task is to set a stage, build a series of events, and move a series of characters through Exposition, Conflict, and final, successful Conclusion.

The Middle Ages was such a period in our Church History. The Lord allowed our Church to suffer corruption and heresies. There was sometimes confusion as to what to believe. Heresies were being expounded by strong figures within the church. Jesus painted these people and events as turbulence, or dark tones on the canvas. But He balanced the dark with the light and radiance of St. Francis of Assisi, St. Dominic, St. Anthony of Padua, and for our purposes in this episode of the Eucharistic Miracle of Bolsena, *St. Thomas Aquinas, defender of the Eucharist.*

Another character of great importance is *Pope Urban IV*, née James Pantaleon. In his younger years, James had been influenced greatly by Blessed Juliana of Liege, a third character in the Eucharistic Miracle. Juliana was a Sister in Liege. From her earliest years, she had been plagued by a vision of the moon, streaked with a black band. She saw this vision day and night. She could not get it out of her mind. Then, she had a vision from Our Lord Jesus in which He explained the meaning of the moon streaked with a black band. Our Lord explained to her that the moon represented the Christian year with all its feasts. The black band represented the one feast which was missing from the Christian Calendar, one in honor of Jesus in the Blessed Sacrament.

After the apparition, she devoted the rest of her life trying to initiate a feast in the Church in honor of the Blessed Sacrament. As is the case with any of God's people who have a devotion to the Blessed Sacrament, Juliana's life was filled with suffering and persecution. She became prioress of her community, and began her quest for a feast day for the Blessed Sacrament. Because of this, she was accused of stealing, misappropriations of funds, and was thrown out of her community twice. This occurred in spite of support of James Pantaleon and other high ranking members of the Belgian Church. Her life ended in poverty and sickness in 1258, without her having seen this dream realized.

James Pantaleon was elected to Pope Urban IV, and became very involved in the many problems to which the Church was being subjected. But the seed of Jesus, planted by Blessed Juliana, remained in the recesses of his consciousness until the Lord was ready to make it grow.

In the Eleventh and Twelfth Centuries, a particular heresy, Berengarianism became very strong throughout Europe. It denied the true presence of Jesus in the Eucharist. It gathered strength, and was followed by false mysticism, pantheism and free love movements. It was being accepted by many of the intelligentsia within the Church, who were in turn spreading it to the people.

This brings us to the last character in Our Lord's drama, who appeared like a bright star that streaked across the sky, disappearing as quickly as it had appeared. This was a priest, called *Peter of Prague*. He was the catalyst that produced the event, which brought all these people together, and accomplished the Lord's Goal.

In 1263, Peter of Prague seemed to appear out of nowhere, and once the miracle had occurred, he disappeared, and was never heard from again. He was having great doubts about the physical presence of Jesus in the Eucharist. Peter was a good man, of great virtue. He was traveling on Pilgrimage towards Rome. He hoped that by praying at the tomb of his namesake, St. Peter, and at the tomb of one of the greatest sources of strength of our Church, St. Paul, he would be filled with the faith he needed to remain in his ministry.

On his way to Rome, he stopped for the night at the little village of Bolsena, about 70 miles north of Rome. He stayed at the Church of Santa Christina, a local heroine saint of the early days of the church. He had heard about the miraculous altar of the saint, and asked to celebrate Mass at that altar. He was looking for all the help he could get. He knew only one way to ask. He had faith, but he didn't know it. He didn't go outside the church for help. He didn't look to humans for help. He knew that the only way he could regain his faith, become whole, was through Our Lord Jesus. So the following morning, he did the only thing he knew how to do. He went to the altar of St. Christina to celebrate the Mass.

As had become his custom, he prayed before the Mass for the grace which would give him faith. He prayed fervently to God. His prayer was the same. He begged for the faith to believe without any doubt that the gift we had been given at the Last Supper, that he had been given on the day of his ordination, was truly the Body of Christ. At the time of the Consecration of the Mass, he elevated the host high above his head, and said the words of consecration. As he said "THIS IS MY BODY", the unleavened bread turned into Flesh, and began to bleed profusely. The blood fell onto the Corporal. The priest, shocked, and not knowing exactly

what to do, wrapped the host in the Corporal, folded the Corpo-
ral, and left the Altar. As he left, drops of blood spilled on the
marble floor in front of the altar.

Pope Urban IV (James Pantaleon) was in Orvieto at the
time, which is a short distance from Bolsena. We begin to see
the Lord's plan unfold. Peter of Prague immediately went off to
tell him what had happened. There's nothing recorded in history
to tell us what went on in the mind of our Pope when this
priest came to him. Had this burning of Blessed Juliana for a
feast day in honor of the Blessed Sacrament stayed with him all
through the years? Did he get a flashback of his younger days
with her?

We do know what he did. He immediately sent a bishop
back to Bolsena to speak to the priests at the church, in order to
verify what Peter of Prague had told him, and bring back to
Orvieto the Sacred Host and Corporal. We also know that the
Pope didn't wait for the Bishop to return. He, followed by the
entire population of Orvieto, went out to meet the Bishop. They
met at a place called the Bridge of the Sun. When he saw the
Eucharistic Miracle, Pope Urban IV went down on his knees at
the sight of his Lord manifested before him in physical form on
the Sacred Corporal.

The Pope had already made his decision, or perhaps the
decision had been given to him by the Lord, that this was truly
a miracle. He received the Miraculous Corporal from the
Bishop and brought It back to Orvieto. He went to the balcony
of the Papal Palace, raised It reverently, showing It to the people of the town. Proclaiming that the Lord had truly visited His
people, he declared that the Eucharistic Miracle of Bolsena
truly dispelled the heresies that had been running rampant.

At about this time, a follower of Blessed Juliana's contacted the Pope through a Bishop in Liege. She repeated the request of Blessed Juliana for a feast day in honor of the Blessed
Sacrament. We are not sure of the sequence of events. Assuming that Pope Urban IV had been given the inspiration to insti-

The reliquary containing the Blood-stained Corporal and the Chapel in Orvieto where the Corporal is venerated.

tute the feast of Corpus Christi solely as a result of the Eucharistic Miracle of Bolsena, this additional prodding by the Lord might possibly have been what was needed to convince him. We do know that throughout the next year the Pope occupied himself almost exclusively to the task of writing the Papal Bull, *Transiturus,* which was published on August 11, 1264. That Papal Bull instituted the Feast of Corpus Christi, in honor of the Blessed Sacrament.

Enter *St. Thomas Aquinas.* When the Pope made the decision to create this new feast in honor of the Blessed Sacrament, he asked St. Thomas Aquinas to write the Liturgy for the Mass. The Hymns created for this feast are considered to be among the greatest in our Church. *O Salutaris* and *Tantum Ergo* are two of the beautiful hymns composed by St. Thomas for this feast.

But that's not all. Our Lord Jesus had a very special reason to get St. Thomas Aquinas involved in the Eucharistic Miracle of Bolsena, and the Feast of Corpus Christi. St. Thomas was a brilliant member of the Body of Christ. In 1269, St. Louis IX, King of France, asked for St. Thomas to settle an argument among the members of the University of Paris. What argument would that be but the physical presence of Jesus in the Eucharist.

St. Thomas prayed fervently, because he realized that he was but an instrument of the Lord, and that an answer that would satisfy intellectuals would have to come from divine inspiration, rather than from his own mind. After much prayer, he wrote a treatise which was first accepted by the University, and then later by the whole church. After having written this treatise, we're told that he received an apparition from Our Dear Lord Jesus. In this apparition, Our Lord said to him: "You have written well of the Sacrament of My Body." At this, St. Thomas went into an ecstasy, and levitated. He was above the ground so long that many of his associates were able to witness the levitation.

This is by no means the end of the story, but it does conclude the series of events the Lord put into motion many years before when he gave the sign on the moon to Blessed Juliana of Liege.

In Bolsena the pieces of marble on which the blood spilled were taken up from the floor of the altar, and placed into reliquaries. There are four stones, each showing the blood of the Sacred Host. Three of them were placed in a special altar, called the Altar of the Miracle, in the Church of Bolsena. The fourth one was placed in a special reliquary, which was built later on. It was placed on the wall behind the original altar of St. Christina, where the miracle took place. Each year, on the feast of the miracle, this reliquary is carried through the town in solemn procession.

There was a phenomenal occurrence regarding the stones of Bolsena. It was assumed that the blood had stained the marble floor, and what was seen was on top of the marble. It is well known that liquid can't penetrate marble. It beads on top, and stains marble. A priest came to Bolsena to request a piece of the Sacred Marble to use as a relic for the altar of a new church that was being built. When the officials of the church attempted to chip off a piece of the stone to give to the priest, they found that the blood had indeed penetrated the marble, causing it to become a part of the marble. Needless to say, they didn't give the piece of marble to the priest for the new church, nor have they given any pieces of the sacred stone to anyone to this day.

The new chapel dedicated to the Eucharistic Miracle of Bolsena is off to the left of the main altar in this very antique church. There is a deacon there who allows pilgrims to witness the Sacred Marble pieces, which are on the altar behind thin panes of glass. He tells the story of the miracle, as well as other reported miracles over the years. One better known local miracle that he tells about is that at various times throughout the years individuals and groups of people have been known to see the face of Our Lord Jesus on the stones. These people have also reported receiving sudden healings.

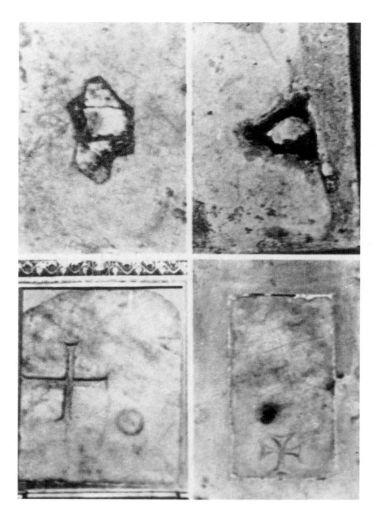

The marble stones at Bolsena showing the Stains of Christ's Blood.

A Papal Bull was written by Pope Gregory X on September 11, 1272. Indulgences were granted to faithful who venerated the Eucharistic shrine at Bolsena. He is also responsible for a new Church being built. Pope Paul VI visited the shrine in 1976, and raised it to the level of a Minor Basilica. He verified the miracle, and reiterated the indulgences granted by his predecessor.

The Church is named in honor of St. Christina, a Virgin Martyr of the early Church, and also the Patron Saint of Bolsena. She was a young girl of fourteen when she embraced Our Lord Jesus and the Christian Faith. Her father, Urbanus, was Prefect of the city, whose job among other things, was to kill and torture Christians. He was very upset when he learned of her conversion. He was more than upset when she smashed all the gold and silver images of gods in their home, and sold the gold and silver to give the money to the poor.

Urbanus was a just man. He loved his daughter Christina very much. First he pleaded with her to deny Christianity, this new religion. When all his persuasion failed, he had no choice but to treat her in the same way he treated other Christians. Though his heart was heavy, he beat her, tied a large stone around her neck, and threw her into Lake Bolsena. The tradition is that all the water in the lake was absorbed by the stone, and Christina was found standing in the empty lake on the stone, her feet imprinted in the rock. That rock is embedded in the altar of St. Christina, where the Eucharistic Miracle took place.

Many other tortures were inflicted upon Christina, which had no effect on her, including cutting off her tongue and her breasts, being thrown into a vat of boiling oil, submitting to the bite of venomous snakes, and other atrocities. She finally succumbed to an arrow which was thrust into her heart. She died in the year 303 a.d.

There are in the church, catacombs, dating back to the early Christian times, where St. Christina was originally buried.

The Miracle of the Eucharist occurred on the altar of St. Christina, where her remains are now buried. There are many beautiful sculptures there, done by the famous Italian, Della Robbia.

There is a very special priest at the Church of Bolsena, Monsignor Don Giacomo Puri. He is the custodian of the Shrine of the Miracle of Bolsena. Msgr. Puri is a very spiritual man, who has devoted his life to the Miracle of Bolsena. Much of the information about this church and its background, as well as material on the Eucharistic Miracle of Bolsena, was given to us by him. He took us on a tour of the shrine, explaining in detail the events of the miracle. He also is responsible for a small Guide Book of the Basilica, which is written in English, French, Italian and German.

In Orvieto a Cathedral was erected immediately. Again, we are witness to the Lord's power. When He wants something done, it gets done. The old Cathedral, Santa Maria de Vescovado, was in a shambles. Rain was coming through the roof, and grass was growing in between the cracks of the pavement. Major ceremonies had been transferred to other churches, because nobody wanted to use the run down old Cathedral.

Pope Urban IV took up residence at Orvieto in 1261, and stayed there until 1264. Prior to the Eucharistic Miracle in 1263, not enough interest could be worked up among the wealthy people of Orvieto to finance a new Cathedral. After the miracle, funds began pouring in almost immediately. They couldn't house the magnificent Eucharistic Miracle in a broken down Cathedral. Plans were drawn up and work began. In 1281, a rich Cardinal died during a visit to Orvieto. In his will, he asked for his tomb to be built in an exquisite church; and left the money to do it. The Cathedral was on its way.

When it was completed in 1310, an entire side chapel was devoted to the Eucharistic Miracle of Bolsena. A reliquary of gilded silver, decorated with translucent enamels, was constructed for the Eucharistic Corporal. It was placed in a marble tabernacle above the altar in the chapel. There are paintings on all the walls of the chapel, telling stories of various Eucharistic Miracles. On the right wall, the entire story of Bolsena and Orvieto, including the declaration of the Papal Bull verifying the Eucharistic Miracle, is depicted. On the left wall are depicted various other Eucharistic Miracles.

The Eucharistic Miracle of Bolsena shows the power of the Lord in many ways. In researching the events and people involved, at first it seemed rather disjointed. We read about the miracle, and found that Pope Urban IV and Thomas Aquinas were involved. In researching Pope Urban IV, we became aware of Blessed Juliana of Liege, and her vision of the Moon. We also found that James Pantaleon, who later became Pope Urban IV, was greatly influenced by Blessed Juliana. If that was not enough, we came to realize that Thomas' role was much greater than writing the Liturgy of the Feast. He used all that he had learned about the Eucharist as a result of the Miracle of Bolsena in his treatise five years later in Paris, to defend the Eucharist.

As a plot for a movie, or mini-series on television, or a novel, the events leading up to the Eucharistic Miracle of Bolsena would be considered too contrived. And yet, as far as we can tell, the Lord's plan was instituted 60 years prior to the miracle, in a city at the easternmost part of Belgium, with the birth of Blessed Juliana of Liege. The instrument he used as a catalyst was a priest from Prague, which is a great distance from Bolsena, Italy. If it were not the Lord's plan, it would be too outrageous to be considered plausible.

We mentioned before about limiting the powers of God, of putting Him into a box. The Eucharistic Miracle of Bolsena and Orvieto is a perfect example that the Lord's power is not limited, and He certainly does not allow Himself to be put in a box.

Siena, 1730: He Shall Live Forever

As we visit the shrines of the various Eucharistic Miracles in the World, the custodians invariably tell us that *their* Eucharistic Miracle is the most important. They then proceed to tell us why they believe that this is so. Their arguments are usually very convincing.

Whether one Eucharistic Miracle is more important than another is not for us to question. For us every Eucharistic Miracle, be it the miracle of the Consecration which takes place on every altar in the world every day, or a specially chosen Eucharistic Miracle, such as those we're writing about in this book, is a *tremendous miracle*, one that should have us down on our knees in veneration.

We have always needed help with our faith. Thomas the Apostle, Doubting Thomas, is a mirror of all of us. He had to see in order to believe. The Lord praises those who have not seen and yet believe. But it's so difficult. In Chapter 11 of Hebrews, the author tells us "Faith is confident assurance concerning what we hope for, and conviction about things we do not see." He spends the rest of that chapter telling us about our ancestors, from Abel down to Moses, all having faith in the commands the Lord gave them. Then he tells us that none of them ever lived to see the promises the Lord had made to them. But they obeyed Him anyway, believing without seeing, making the journey, knowing that the promises made would be fulfilled.

To be sure, there were times when their great faith lagged, and became bogged down with uncertainty and doubt. It was at these times that the Lord gave them special signs to help them in their doubt and disbelief. He has not changed His style. He does the same for us.

One of the great signs He gave us in the form of a Eucharistic Miracle took place in 1730 in the City of Siena, in Italy. Siena has always been a place of great art and culture. Some consider it an overflow from Florence, but the Siennese would tell you then, and will tell you now, that Siena has its own background of culture and art, which is completely independent of Florence, or for that matter, anywhere else.

One might question, Why Siena? Why in 1730? What was the significance? Siena is famous for its most well known citizen, St. Catherine, born almost 400 years before the Eucharistic Miracle. In her short 33 years, she made a lasting impact on the Church, and did more to make Siena known the world over than any of the great cultural or artistic gifts which the Lord has given us through this town. She is a doctor of the Church, although she had no formal training in reading or writing. She was greatly instrumental in bringing the Popes back from Avignon, France, to Rome. She had the stigmata, and was known to exist for long periods on just the Eucharist for sustenance. She had a great devotion to the presence of Jesus in the Eucharist.

St. Bernardine of Siena is also one of the city's well known inhabitants, almost 300 years before the Eucharistic Miracle. A Franciscan, and reformer of the Franciscan Order, St. Bernardine encouraged devotion to the Eucharist early in his preaching career. As he became well known, thousands of faithful came to listen to his preaching. He always held up a tablet, showing the Eucharist with rays of sun emanating from it, and the symbol IHS in the middle. This came to be known as his symbol. His influence over Italy is evident by the symbol of St.

Bernardine, which can be seen on many buildings in Italy, especially in Siena and Florence.

But Siena in 1730 had changed. It was no longer the Siena of St. Catherine of 400 years before, or the Siena of St. Bernardine of 300 years before. It was a place, like much of Europe, where Feast Days were occasions for celebrating. The religious significance of a Feast like the Assumption, on August 15, was very likely overshadowed by the importance of a day off from work, where the entire town met at the Piazza Del Campo, to celebrate the day rather than the Feast. Everybody went to Church, and many most likely received Communion. But the reasoning may have been more to show off a new outfit, or see who else was there at the Church, than to venerate Our dear Lady's Assumption into Heaven, or marvel at the Miracle of the Eucharist, which took place before their eyes.

Siena in 1730 was ready for a miracle. We in the Church had lost the urgency that existed during the time of St. Francis and St. Dominic. It had been very obvious that the Church, the people of God were desperately in need of immediate reform. But by the middle of the 18th Century, we had become comfortable again. We were very seriously involved in Renaissance. The magic and excitement of our Faith had become old hat. Our interests had given way to Art and Culture. The time was ripe. All of Italy, and indeed Europe needed something to bring them to their knees, and focus their attention back to the power of God. In these instances, our Lord is never lacking.

On the morning of the day before the Feast of the Assumption, the priests in all the churches in Siena consecrated extra Hosts in anticipation of the large crowds who would be receiving Communion the next day. Then they all went over to the magnificent Duomo, the Cathedral, to plan the festivities of the following day, and take part in the Vigil Ceremony that night.

All went as anticipated. The town was virtually abandoned, except for the large congregation at the Cathedral. All the churches were empty. In the afternoon of the 14th, thieves stole into the Basilica of St. Francis, which is on the northern end of town. They broke into the Tabernacle, not for the precious Body of Our Lord Jesus, but for the gold of the Ciborium which held His Body. They took everything with them, Hosts as well as Ciborium. No one was aware of the crime until the following morning when the priests of the Church were about to celebrate Mass for the feast.

Panic set in. Proof of the crime was confirmed when someone brought in the top of the Ciborium which he said he had found in the street outside the church. The entire town went about looking for the lost Hosts. The festivities for the day, so well prepared, were suspended. The Archbishop asked for public prayers for the well being of the Consecrated Hosts, and Their safe return. We must remember here that they didn't know for sure why the Consecrated Hosts were stolen. Was it for the gold of the Ciborium, or for a more diabolic purpose, to desecrate and commit blasphemy against Our Defenseless Savior? Again, the Lord allows Himself to be vulnerable. Again, He puts Himself entirely in our hands.

How long were those three days between the time of the theft and the time they found the Hosts. Three Days, which must have seemed as long as the three days between the Crucifixion and the Resurrection, three days which may have been as a lifetime. But as the sun sets, the sun also rises. And on the third day, August 17, while a man was praying in the Church of St. Mary in Provenzano, a short distance from the Basilica of St. Francis, he noticed something white protruding from the Poor Box near him. It was round, and as the morning sun hit it, it seemed to gleam. He immediately told the priest of the Church, who told the Archbishop, who sent one of his people over to the Church of St. Mary.

When the Archbishop's representative and the priest from the Basilica of St. Francis arrived, they opened the poor box together to find a large amount of Hosts, some stuck in between cobwebs, (the poor box was only opened once a year) and some down in the bottom of the box. They counted them to determine if any were missing. The priest from St. Francis told them the count was correct, 348 whole Hosts, and 6 halves. The priest had consecrated 351 Hosts on the 14th of August.

A sigh of relief and a praise to the Lord was sounded, for two reasons. One was that the Consecrated Hosts had been found, and two that none of Them had been taken. They were able to rule out the motive of desecration, which would have been far more devastating than the theft of a gold ciborium. Our Lord had not been blasphemed.

The fear of desecration may seem like overreacting to us, when, since the advent of Communion in the Hand, we find Consecrated Hosts on the floor of the church, outside the church on the ground, slipped in between the pages of missalettes and on and on. We're reminded of an incident where Mass was said in the dining room of a hotel during a Pilgrimage, and the priest dropped a Consecrated Host. He told the people not to look for it, stating "Our Lord understands". Thank God the people did not understand, and immediately found the Host and consumed It. But we should take it seriously. If we're to be accused of overreacting, so be it. The point to be made is the entire focus of this book. *He's there. He's in that piece of Bread and Cup of Wine. Don't take Him for granted.*

After they found the Consecrated Hosts, they cleaned Them as carefully and thoroughly as possible. Then, the next day, in solemn procession, with a large assemblage of the town following, the Hosts were brought back to the Church of St. Francis, where They were venerated by the faithful.

There's no certain explanation of why the Hosts were not distributed. The most obvious reason could be that, although They were cleaned as much as possible, They could still have been soiled from being in the Poor Box. That's obvious, but not necessarily God's reasoning. He doesn't always use the obvious. Had they been distributed, they would have been gone, and the story would have been told by the local people for a few days, a week at the most, and then back to business as usual, which may not have included things of Our Lord.

God fills our needs. We don't always know what our needs are. But He does. Possibly the best explanation, and possibly His reasoning, is that we needed this physical sign for our own faith, for our own time, for all time. The story of the robbery spread through the surrounding countryside, indeed to many far off parts of Italy. People began to make Pilgrimages to the Church of St. Francis to pray before the Consecrated Hosts. And this was before they knew anything about their being Miraculous.

In situations where Consecrated Hosts have been contaminated in any way, they are not required to be consumed. They can just be left until they deteriorate. At that time, the Real Presence leaves them. So it may have been that the Franciscans had meant to allow the Hosts to be venerated by the Pilgrims until such time as they deteriorated, and that would be the end of it. But it never happened.

Time marched on. Every now and then, an important personage in the Church, be it Bishop or Cardinal, would be allowed to receive one of the Hosts, and the report always came back that They tasted fresh. Fifty years passed. The Hosts had not changed. It was time for an investigation. The head of the Franciscan Community examined the Hosts. He received One. He concluded that the Hosts were fresh. From the years of 1730 to 1780, the count had gone down to 230. At this time, new instructions were given that no one could any longer receive the Hosts, because it was believed that a miracle had occurred.

Nine years later, another investigation took place, this time by the Archbishop of Siena. He included prominent theologians of the time, and officials from the town, who were not part of the Church. They subjected the Hosts to a microscopic test. It was determined that the Hosts had not begun to crumble, or discolor, or deteriorate in any way. It was also verified at this time that these were indeed the same Hosts that had been examined in 1780, and the same Hosts that had been lost and found in 1730.

It was at this time that the Archbishop ordered that a quantity of unconsecrated hosts be placed in an airtight container, hermetically sealed, to be locked up and kept in the Chancery office for ten years. The Miraculous Hosts were kept in a Ciborium, not hermetically sealed in any way, just the way they had been for the prior 59 years. At the end of the ten year period, the box with the unconsecrated hosts was opened in the presence of the Archbishop and various officials. They found that they were mostly discolored, disfigured and deteriorated. They again checked the Miraculous Hosts to find that They were in perfect condition.

In 1815, another test was made, again with microscopes, and with people tasting the Hosts. It was determined that They were still fresh. Again in 1850, the Bishop of Siena ordered a test. Again, it was determined that They were as fresh as the day They were baked. At this investigation, they also checked the unconsecrated hosts which had been put in the airtight box in 1789. There was little left of these hosts. They had turned into powder for the most part. Those which had not deteriorated completely were only small pieces, which had turned into an Ochre color.

At that time it was explained that unleavened bread, of which the Hosts were baked, if kept under normal conditions in a ciborium, as were the Miraculous Hosts, would deteriorate in five years at the very most. That's saying a lot. On the other hand, unleavened bread which was put in any kind of airtight container, such as those unconsecrated hosts submitted to the test of time, would last much longer. In this instance, the reverse occurred. The Miraculous Hosts, which have never been in any kind of hermetically sealed container, had at that time lasted 120 years, while the unconsecrated hosts, placed in the airtight container, deteriorated and disintegrated.

In 1914 we were into the age of modern science, where

miracles were not allowed to stand on the intervention of the Almighty. They had to stand the test of logic and science. Outside scientists, as well as people from within the Church, conducted an investigation. Perhaps a lot of the thinking was "Well, we'll finally put this hoax to rest. After all, this is the 20th Century. We're not in the Dark Ages anymore."

An acid and starch test was performed with fragments. They also tested Them under the scrutiny of microscopes, and tasted Them. It was determined by all that They had a normal amount of starch of roughly sifted wheat flour, and that They were well enough preserved to eat, after 184 years.

In 1922, a large assemblage of Bishops and Church officials from all over the area, investigated the Miraculous Hosts again. It was after the results had been the same as in previous investigations that the Bishops declared officially that they could find no natural reason for the Hosts having remained incorrupt for such a long period of time (192 years at this date). They officially claimed it as a supernatural gift from God.

In 1950, the Miraculous Hosts were transferred from the ciborium They had been housed in, to a beautiful, elaborate reliquary. The Bishops and Church Officials then solemnly processed with the Hosts through the town, and kept Them on display for a time. This may have been a mistake, for it brought the Hosts, or the Reliquary, at any rate, to the attention of yet another thief. On August 5th, 1951, nine days before the Anniversary of the Miraculous Theft, the tabernacle was broken into again. This time the thief was very obvious in what he wanted. He took the gold Reliquary, and threw the Miraculous Hosts on the floor of the chapel. Less than a year later, a new reliquary was made for the Miraculous Hosts, which is where They rest to this day.

On September 14, 1980, Pope John Paul II came to Siena to venerate the Eucharistic Miracle in honor of the 250th Anniversary of the Miracle of the Hosts.

The Eucharistic Miracle of Siena is not on display all the

On September 23, 1950 a team of priests examined the hosts at Siena and transferred them to a new Reliquary (top); on September 14, 1980, John Paul II viewed the Miracle as Fr. Giannini looked on.

time. In the Church of St. Francis, it has a Summer and a Winter Chapel. To the left of the main altar is the Summer Residence of Our Lord. It is a magnificent chapel, in which the Miraculous Hosts are in an elaborate tabernacle. Every Friday evening at 6 p.m., there is a Rosary, followed by a Mass, followed by a Benediction with the Miraculous Hosts. To the right of the main altar, in a smaller chapel, is the winter residence of the King of the World. Because the church is so cold in winter, and the priests cannot stay there all the time, the chapel is locked except for the Mass in the Morning. When the Tabernacle door is open, the Hosts gleam like the King He is, on a Golden Throne.

Fr. Antonio Giannini has been the custodian of the Eucharistic Miracle for many years. He has devoted much of his life to the study of various Eucharistic Miracles throughout the world. "Why," he asks us, "do you think the Eucharistic Miracle of Siena is of such great importance, possibly the most important of the Eucharistic Miracles?" Without minimizing the importance of any of the other Eucharistic Miracles that have come down through the centuries, the Eucharistic Miracle of Siena is an ongoing miracle. The Lord has kept this miracle in His consciousness for 250 years. If He were to take it out of His mind for even an instant, it would deteriorate, and disappear. Fr. Giannini mentions other Eucharistic Miracles that have occurred in the history of the Church, that remained for a time, and then disintegrated. They are no less miracles, but they were meant for a time. When the Lord felt they were no longer needed, they disappeared.

According to Fr. Giannini, this miracle is of great importance to the Faithful, so much so that the Lord kept it in existence in the *original species of unleavened bread*. All the other Eucharistic Miracles which we will write about in this book changed from bread and wine into another form. In Lanciano, the bread and wine turned into Flesh and Blood. In Bolsena, the Host bled, and the blood stained corporal has been left for us. In

Cascia, the Host bled, and became two blood stained pages of a book. But in Siena, the Incorrupt Hosts are still Hosts. We believe that as long as the Hosts are incorrupt, the Real Presence of Jesus remains in them. Siena is a miracle in which The Lord made the decision to stay in this form, in this place, without any break, for over 250 years.

We talked about Faith at the beginning of the narrative on the Eucharistic Miracle of Siena. We have been to the Rosaries on Friday night, followed by the Mass and Benediction with the Miraculous Hosts. Usually, Fr. Giannini gives the Benediction. The Faith of these people who crowd into this Church for the blessing, the Faith of this priest who raises His Lord and God truly present in miraculous form, would be enough to make the greatest non-believer change his mind. We look at a man who has given up his entire life for the things we have been taught, which we believe in. He is the greatest witness to the veracity of this miracle. If it were a sham, what a waste his life would have been. But when you look in this priest's eyes and see the blinding light, you know you're looking at the reflection of Jesus.

Bob and Penny Lord do research with the help of Fr. Antonio Giannini, custodian of the Eucharistic Miracle in Siena (top). Cascia is graced by the incorrupt body of St. Rita.

Cascia, 1300's:
The Face of the Savior

Our Journey takes us to the top of a high mountain town, Cascia, in the Umbrian Valley of Italy. Umbria boasts 20,000 saints within her boundaries. Some of the most famous are St. Francis of Assisi, St. Clare of Assisi, St. Veronica Giuliana, Blessed Margaret Castello, St. Benedict, founder of the Benedictine Order, born in Norcia, and St. Rita of Cascia.

When one speaks of the miracle of Cascia, one cannot leave out St. Rita. The life of St. Rita is fascinating. She is such a modern saint. She's called the Saint of the Impossible. She was an obedient daughter, a faithful wife, an abused wife, a mother, a widow, a religious, a Stigmatist, and an incorrupt saint. St. Rita experienced it all.

She wanted to be a nun all her life. Her parents, however, were concerned for her. They had had her late in life, and felt it best that she marry before they die. Their choice of a husband was a poor one, but Rita obeyed. After the marriage, her husband proved to be a drinker, a carouser, and a wife beater. Rita remained faithful to him all their married life. They also had two children, who took the father's temperament. Rita worried about this, and prayed for them.

After twenty years of marriage and prayer on the part of St. Rita, the husband was converted. He begged forgiveness from Rita for his past life, and vowed to change his ways. He gave up his drinking and carousing, and spent his time with Rita, and in prayer. This did not last too long, however, because while her husband Paolo had reformed, his former friends and enemies had not. One night Paolo didn't come home. Prior to his conversion, this would not have been unusual, but for the reformed Paolo, this was serious. Rita knew something was wrong. The next day, he was found murdered.

Her grief was compounded when her two sons, now of age, vowed to avenge the death of their father. No amount of pleading could dissuade them. Rita pleaded with the Lord to save the souls of her two children. She asked Him to take their lives rather than let them lose their souls by committing mortal sin. In this, the Lord answered her prayers. Both were stricken with a fatal illness. During their time of illness, she spoke softly to them of love and forgiveness. By the time they died, they had forgiven their father's murderers. Rita was convinced at the time that they were with their father in heaven.

Now that she was truly alone, she reached out to the Augustinian sisters to allow her the vocation she had prayed for as a child. But that was not to be easy in coming. They didn't want a woman who had been married. Her husband's violent death left a shadow of doubt. Her sons wanted to engage in vendetta. This did not speak well of her as a mother. She turned again to Jesus in prayer. He interceded in a physical miracle which the Augustinian nuns could not deny. Based on that, she was allowed to become a nun.

She was given the gift of the Stigmata, marks of the Crown of Thorns in her head. When most saints have been given this gift, their heavenly wounds have the fragrance of heaven (a very sweet smelling aroma). Padre Pio had it; St. Francis of Assisi had it; Fr. Gino has it. Rita's wounds smelled so putrid that she had to be kept away from people. For 15 years, she lived by herself, away from her sister nuns. The Lord gave her one respite from this, when she wanted to go to Rome for the First Holy Year. Jesus removed the Stigmata from her head for the duration of the Pilgrimage. As soon as she arrived back home from Rome, it reappeared, and she had to be isolated again.

She was many things during her lifetime, but most of all, she was a mother. As she lay on her deathbed, she asked for a sign from the Lord that her sons were with Him in heaven. In the middle of the winter, He gave her a rose from the rose garden near her home in Roccaporena. You would think that would have been enough. She asked for a second sign. Again, He gave her a sign, a fig out of a garden at her home in Roccaporena, again in the dead of winter.

She seems to have triumphed in death. When she died, the wound of the Stigmata left her, to be replaced by a ruby red spot, which had the most delightful fragrance. She was supposed to be laid out in the convent, but there was such a crowd to pay their last respects to her that they had to put her inside the church. She stayed there for many days, and the fragrance never left her. Because of this, she was never buried. The wooden casket originally meant for her, was replaced by a glass casket, and she has been on display for the faithful to venerate from that time to this.

This small town of Cascia, which hosts the incorrupt body of this great saint, high above the tree line and near the cloud line, has become famous. A special church was built for her after the guns of World War II quieted. As you enter the church, there is the anticipation of venerating the incorrupt body of the saint. Because of that, we become preoccupied, and have tunnel vision. We are looking for St. Rita, and see nothing beyond that shrine.

But if pilgrims who come to this church would take time to look at the stained glass windows surrounding the main altar, and those in the chapel directly across from the chapel of the saint, they would have to ask themselves a question, as our grandson asked us one year. Why are there so many Eucharistic Miracles depicted on the Stained Glass Windows? Around the main altar are shown the Miracles of Bolsena/Orvieto, Lanciano, St. Anthony and the Donkey, St. Clare of Assisi and the Saracens, and the Multiplication of the Loaves and Fishes.

Our grandson noticed that there was another stained glass window, one we didn't recognize. The stained glass window depicted an open book, with two round red spots on the pages facing each other. Knowing most of the symbols of the Eucharistic Miracles, he asked us what that stained glass window represented. We said it was probably just a symbol, because we didn't know what it stood for. That was not good enough for him. He kept after us until we asked a nun at the church to explain what it meant. Her explanation and my grandson's insistence, gave us the gift of the Eucharistic Miracle of Cascia.

In the chapel on the opposite side of the church, to the right as you enter, is an altar with a tabernacle, which contains the Eucharistic Miracle of Cascia. Beneath the tabernacle is a glass case with the bones of one Blessed Simone Fidati, who was involved in this Eucharistic Miracle. Fr. Simone was an Augustinian priest during the middle Fourteenth Century. He was very well known throughout the Umbria, as a holy and wise man, despite the fact that he was very young. Because of his great piety and wisdom, it was a normal occurrence for other priests to search him out to confess their sins. While Blessed Simone was stationed at the Augustinian monastery in Siena, a priest came to him one day, to make this unusual confession.

He had lost his respect for the Eucharist. From that we would have to gather that he could not possibly have believed that Our Lord Jesus came to us in the Eucharist, or he could not have lost his respect. Apathy can be a powerful weapon for Satan. There was no excitement left in this priest's life. He went through the motions. He did what he had to, but had become more and more withdrawn from God and his congregation. Perhaps he had begun to take Jesus in the Eucharist and Jesus in his people for

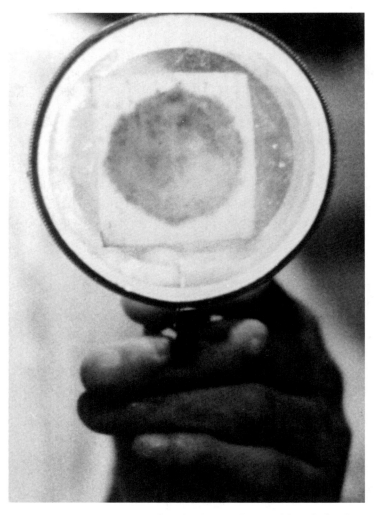

The bloodstained page at Cascia shows the profile of the face of Christ. Barely traceable in this picture, the face is more clearly visible on the actual page.

granted.

This priest was called on a Sick Call. Rather than put the Eucharist in a pyx, and carry it close to his heart, our priest took the Host, threw it irreverently between the pages of his Breviary, and went on the sick call. When he arrived at the home of the sick man, he prepared him to receive the Eucharist. He opened the book to take out the Host to give the sick man Communion. On opening the book to where the Host had been, the priest was shocked to find in its place two round bloodstains on the pages facing each other. The priest left the house in a panic, and immediately sought out Blessed Simone, who was known for his sanctity.

Blessed Simone, listening to the priest's account of his sin and the miracle, gave him absolution. But he took the two bloodstained pages from him. One of them was put in a tabernacle in Perugia, and the other in an Augustinian monastery in Cascia.

The Eucharistic Miracle has been venerated over the years in the Augustinian Monastery of Cascia. It was verified by the local bishop. It has been carried in solemn procession during the Feast of Corpus Christi. Special indulgences have been granted by the Pope for those who venerate the Eucharistic Miracle.

In 1930, a Eucharistic Congress was held at Norcia, close to Cascia. At that time, a beautiful Monstrance was made to hold the Eucharistic Miracle. It was in honor of the 6th Centennial of the miracle. When the new church in honor of St. Rita was built, adjacent to the Augustinian monastery, a special chapel was built for the Eucharistic Miracle.

There is a singular phenomenon attributed to this miracle. Or could it be a miracle within a miracle? Over the years, people began to notice a change in the bloodstained page. A face began to take shape on the page. It's almost as if darker coloration gravitated to certain places on the page. There are those who can look at the page and see the face of Christ. When the priest at the shrine opens up the tabernacle to show the faithful the Eucharistic Miracle, he puts on vestments, as if he were going to celebrate Mass. As he brings the Monstrance to the Altar railing, he puts a flashlight in back of the page, so that the face shows through. It is a perfectly formed profile of a man with a beard and a mustache.

Over the years, the Church has been criticized for too much ritual, hocus pocus, supernatural nonsense, even from within, and perhaps especially from within. In an effort to achieve acceptance from a non-supernatural world that would have us break our faith down to a human equation, many of our own have rejected the beautiful gifts we have been given in the form of divine intervention. Many, in their attempt to touch upon the Humanity of Jesus, are forgetting about or rejecting His Divine Nature. He is the Second Person of the Trinity, God the Son.

If we praise Him for loving us so much that He was willing to lower Himself to become one of us, we give Him glory. But if we bring Him and all His works down to our human level, we've lost everything along the way. We've lost our beautiful Tradition, our Faith in the promises of Jesus fulfilled, and yet to be fulfilled. We've lost God.

Macerata, 1356:
Broken and Bleeding

Fr. Antonio Giannini, the custodian of the Shrine of the Incorrupt Hosts of Siena, possesses wealth of information on every Eucharistic Miracle known to the Church. It was because of his love for the Eucharist, and his excitement about the various shrines dedicated to Miracles of the Eucharist, that we began to visit these shrines. Fr. Giannini was not as fortunate as we, in that he was not able to travel all over Europe to see in person the places and miracles he had committed to memory. We became, in effect, his eyes and ears. Each time we returned to Siena, we shared in great detail our experiences at the shrines of the Eucharist we had visited since the last time we had been with him. We documented these trips with photographs wherever possible. He, in turn, expounded on what we had learned, by explaining the significance of the miracles during the time that they happened, as well as the importance in the Church today.

We mention Fr. Giannini here in contrast with another Franciscan we met at Loreto, the shrine of the Holy House of Nazareth, which is about 20 miles from Macerata. This young Franciscan had been born in Macerata. We were planning to visit the Eucharistic Miracle in that town, and asked the young man to tell us about it, and where in the town it was located. He knew absolutely nothing about the miracle. He spent about twenty minutes trying to convince us that there was no Eucharistic Miracle in the town of his birth.

When we arrived at Macerata, we almost didn't find the shrine to the Eucharistic Miracle. The young Franciscan who was born in this town was right about one thing. Not very many people know about it.

There is a well known shrine in Macerata, to Our Lady of Mercy of Macerata. Her small church, or chapel, is right outside the Cathedral. Inside her little church there is a painting of Our Lady of Mercy. The church has been credited with saving the population of Macerata from a pestilence in 1447.

In that year, all of Italy was victimized by a plague, which was killing the population in massive proportions. The Town Council had a meeting and passed a very unusual law. As a prayer of petition to Our Lady, they decided that they would build a little church in 24 hours. They chose the Feast of the Assumption, August 15, to construct the church. Everybody in the town took part in the project. There were city officials, clergy, nobility, peasants, all with one goal. Within 24 hours, the chapel was built. As a reward, Our Lady interceded with Jesus and the town of Macerata was spared. Fifty years later, a proper church was built. But it wasn't until 1721 that the Vatican honored Our Lady of Macerata with a Crown. At that time a new church was built, which is today a beautiful shrine to Our Lady of Mercy of Macerata. It has become a very important Marian Pilgrimage Shrine for the area, the Marches.

The Franciscan who was the custodian of this shrine to Our Lady had heard something about a Eucharistic Miracle, but had never seen it. He told us to speak to Msgr. Gentili, who was sure to know the details of the miracle, and where it could be found. We would like to give special thanks to Msgr. Gentili. He was ill the day we visited the Cathedral, and yet he gave us all the time we needed, and all the information he could about the miracle.

There are no records available documenting the Eucharistic Miracle. They were lost many years ago. There is a parchment attached to the Eucharistic Miracle, attesting to its authenticity. The story of the Eucharistic Miracle is written on this parchment which dates back to the 14th century.

The priest who was celebrating the Mass on the day of the Eucharistic Miracle of Macerata had an unusual problem. While it's believed that he had doubts as to the Real Presence of Jesus in the Eucharist, at this Mass in which Our Lord made Himself physically present the priest was not sure whether Our Lord Jesus remained equally in the fractions of the Host when It was broken. In the normal course of events, after the Consecration, but before the priest consumes the Big Host, he breaks it, and then puts a small portion into the Chalice containing the Blood of Jesus.

We had never heard about this doubt on the part of our priests before, but Msgr. Gentili told us that it has been debated in the Church for centuries, and has been written about by St. Thomas Aquinas.

Given this background, let us go to the day of the miracle, to the Consecration of the Mass. The priest was having his doubts as to whether Jesus was equally present in the fractions of the Host. As he broke the Host, Blood began pouring out of the Host, into the Chalice. It probably would have all poured into the Chalice, had not the priest panicked. His hands started to shake, indeed his whole body. He lost control of himself. The blood fell onto the Corporal, and consequently onto the Altar Cloth.

The priest immediately went to the Bishop Nicolo di San Martino, and explained what had happened. The Bishop ordered the incident investigated, after which he gave it his seal of approval. The Miraculous Corporal was placed in the Cathedral of Macerata in a position of prominence. The entire population adored Our Lord Jesus in this miracle. Each year, It was

The Altarcloth at Macerata where the Blood fell during the Consecration of the Mass.

brought through the streets of the city in procession, on the first Sunday after Pentecost. Not only the people of Macerata attended the processions, but the entire province came out for them.

This custom was continued down through the years, until the time of Napoleon's conquest of Italy, in 1807. All religious processions, as well as the various Religious Orders, were banned. The Sacred Corporal was locked up in a closet in the Cathedral for over 100 years, forgotten. In 1932, it was taken out again, and placed in a position of importance in the Cathedral. However, shortly after, with the coming of the Second World War, Facism and Nazism, the Corporal went back into the closet. For a few years after the war ended, the Eucharistic Miracle was carried in procession on the Feast of Corpus Christi, in back of the Blessed Sacrament.

Today it is kept under the Altar of the Blessed Sacrament in the Cathedral of Macerata. It is covered up by an Altar Board. On the Feast of Corpus Christi, It is taken out and venerated near the main altar. The blood stains, now over 600 years old, can still be distinguished on the Corporal. But they are dull and colorless. We don't know why the Lord has allowed this special Gift of Himself in the form of His Blood to become obscured and forgotten. Perhaps He is waiting for a time when there will be a great need on the part of the people for a miracle of this magnitude to be revived.

Interestingly, Macerata is also a place of Pilgrimage for Our Lady. Many Italian Pilgrims include Macerata in Pilgrimages to Loreto, in petition and thanksgiving. So it is a very active shrine. The people of the town have been very fervent in support of veneration of this shrine.

Bagno di Romagna, 1412: Living Blood

We often wonder why Our Lord Jesus or His Mother Mary pick the places they do to perform miracles or make apparitions. Bagno di Romagna is a sleepy little village way up in the mountains between Arezzo and Cesena, Italy. If you were to go there from Forli, or Cesena, near the Adriatic Sea, it's a pleasant ride up the mountain, taking about 40 minutes. If you go from Arezzo, it's a curvy mountainous, hair-pin-turn-take-your-life-in-your-hands ride. It's a pretty little town, not overly affected by the fact that Our Lord presented Himself to the people of this town in a Physical way, close to 600 years ago, in the year 1412.

The church of Santa Maria Assunta, now a Basilica, was originally built over a pagan temple. It has fluctuated from church to monastery over the years. At the time of the miracle, it was a Monastery called the Abbey Camaldolese of Santa Maria in Bagno under the custodianship of a Fr. Lazarro and the Camaldolese Monks.

This priest was having problems with his Faith. The problems that existed at the time of Lanciano, or Bolsena or Siena have existed from the first days of our Church, and continue until today. However, we have had the gift from the beginning that the Lord gave us, "Know that I am always with you, until the end of the world" Matt 28: 20. We believe that at these times, when we are in such need of Him, He comes to us in this very special way, in miracle Form so that we will remember these words He gave us.

But on this day (we don't know the date), our priest was having a particularly bad attack of uncertainty about physical presence of Our Lord Jesus in the Eucharist. He was being plagued by the most diabolic thoughts. He began the Celebration of the Mass. He could not shake the powers that were overcoming him. But he continued on. During the Consecration, the pressure became unbearable. He was losing the little faith he had left. Suddenly, as he peered into the chalice, he couldn't believe his eyes. The wine turned into red blood, and began to boil. It spurted out of the Chalice and onto the Corporal. It was alive, throbbing.

Why did the blood throb? All of the writings we have translated emphasize that It was alive. The priest we interviewed when we visited the miracle at the Church talked about "The Living Blood". Perhaps it was necessary to impress on the priest the truth of the Living God. By having the blood boil, throb, pulsate, this dear priest would be convinced that His God was truly alive in the presence of the Blood. Maybe it was for other priests, other people within or outside of the Church, for then, for now.

In all the Eucharistic Miracles that we've studied and visited, the Lord uses a unique way to manifest Himself to us. This, the Eucharistic Miracle of Bagno di Romagna, is one of the most unusual that we've experienced.

The priest was visibly shaken when this happened. He turned to the congregation in tears, sobbing a confession of his sin of doubt, and the gift that the Lord had given him. He prayed for forgiveness, and vowed his lifetime faith in the physical presence of Our Lord Jesus in the Eucharist. It had a permanent effect on his life. He led an exemplary life for the next five years, after which he died. When he died, he was given the title "Venerable" because of the pious life he had lived from the time of the miracle until his death.

It was 365 years later that the blood stained corporal was transferred to a silver reliquary. Pope Pius VI convened a commission to study the facts of the incident. On August 25, 1777, the corporal was transferred. But it was still not on display for the public to venerate. In 1885, a local bishop from San Sepolcro opened the silver container and examined the bloodstained corporal. He confirmed that the spots of blood were still clear and red.

For the five hundredth anniversary, in 1912, a large celebration was held in honor of the miracle. It was tied in with a Eucharistic Study for a week, which was attended by over a hundred priests.

Another investigation was performed on the Blood Stained Corporal in 1958. This time, scientific means were used. A chemical analysis was done at the University of Florence. It was confirmed that the corporal held real blood. Considering the explanation we gave at the beginning of the book, that blood loses its chemical qualities very shortly after it is shed, this is another very important Eucharistic Miracle, in that it still retains the properties of blood, after almost 600 years.

The Sacred Corporal is kept in a reliquary in the Church of Santa Maria Assunta in Bagno in a special chapel, constructed specifically to accommodate the Corporal. The reliquary has a glass front allowing us to see the blood stains on the corporal. It is not on display at all times, but on special occasions during the year. However, It can be made available for pilgrims. The pastor of the church, although he only speaks Italian, is more than happy to relate the story of the miracle to any Pilgrim group, as he did for us.

Let us talk for a minute about the greatest aspect of this miracle, probably the main reason the Lord decided to manifest Himself in this way, the conversion of this one priest. What does this tell us? For one thing, it tells us how important the royal priesthood is to Our Lord. Jesus, the great shepherd, aware of the problems of one of the least of His children, comes down to Earth in the physical manifestation of His Blood, to restore the faith, and save the vocation of this one man.

It tells us that Jesus is with us, as He promised in Matthew 28:20. Out of the billions of people on earth, He is aware of every tear that drops, every doubt, every fear of every one of His people. Whenever we are low, down at the bottom, we can rise to the top in the knowledge that we are never alone.

That may be the most obvious reason. But there's a greater lesson to be learned from the Eucharist, as manifested in this miracle. There were *two miracles* that took place on that day in 1412, and we're not suggesting that one was greater than the other. The first miracle is that of Our Lord Jesus coming to us in the form of Living Blood. But the other miracle, which we've only touched on, is the Miracle of the Conversion of the Priest, through the Body of Christ. Why did Jesus leave us His Body? His Body, bread converted into Flesh and Blood, calls us to conversion, to change, to Incarnation.

In the Eucharist, change comes about. The bread and wine is changed into the Body and Blood of Our Lord Jesus. But that's only half the change. We have to change, also. Conversion must come about in us. God extends His Hand. All we have to do is reach out and take it.

Some years ago at a Mass during a large Marriage Encounter Convention, the priest told us, "If the only change that happens here is on the Altar, we've wasted the Lord's time, and our own time." The Mass is not a Spectator Sport. The reason it was changed into the vernacular was for us, the Mystical Body of Christ, to take part in it. The Eucharist is the climax of the experience in which humanity joins with Divinity to form a new creation, a New Adam & Eve, a New World. God does His part. We must do ours.

But the people of Bagno di Romagna did not do their part,

Fr. Antonio Moscone is custodian of the Sacred Corporal at Bagno di Romagna, shown here in its Reliquary.

and Our Lord intervened again, this time through His Mother.

In the Church of Santa Maria Assunta at Bagno di Romagna, there is a shrine to Our Lady which receives almost as much attention from the people as the Eucharistic Miracle. It has to do with miraculous intervention also. It is called *Madonna del Sangue*, Our Lady of the Blood. There is an engraving of Our Lady with the Baby Jesus, which is venerated in its own chapel.

In the year 1498, 86 years after the Eucharistic Miracle had occurred in the Church, there was a lot of fighting going on between neighbors in the town of Bagno. There were mistrust, violence and vendettas. In many instances, blood was shed. It doesn't seem possible in a place like Bagno, where the Lord had given the people the gift of Himself in this miraculous form, that anyone could possibly go back to a former way of life. We're reminded of the words of the Curé of Ars, St. John Vianney, as he was about to meet the Lord. He had spent his entire life, working 18 hours a day in the confessional, and teaching his people. He had managed to convert his entire village, as well as much of the surrounding area of France. He said "I know that when I die, they will all go back to the way they were." And after he died, the town did go back to its former ways. So it was with Bagno di Romagna.

There was, in a private home, a woodcut of Our Lady with the Baby Jesus in her Arms. The tradition of the family who owned the engraving was that every night at about 5:30, someone would light a lamp by the woodcut, and pray to Our Lady. On the 20th of January, 1498, one of the children, Bozio Deiaiuti, lit the lamp, and began to pray. He saw blood flowing from the left arm of the woodcut, down the arm. He immediately called his brother Paolo to witness the sight. Paolo reacted naturally. Upon seeing the blood, he promptly fainted.

Word went out quickly to the entire town, and before long, there were great throngs of local people coming to the house to witness the miracle. A greater miracle occurred while the people gathered before the woodcut. They began asking forgiveness of each other for past faults, arguments, vendettas. Within two hours from the time the bleeding began, it stopped. Almost everybody in Bagno who had resentments towards others had seen the miracle, and made amends. Only two had not seen the miracle, Santa and Lucrezia, who had sworn lifelong enmities with each other and their families. When they came into the house, although the bleeding had stopped, two drops of blood flowed from the arm in the presence of these two mortal enemies, causing them to ask forgiveness of each other. With this, the entire town was reconciled to each other.

A few days later, the Abbot of the Church brought the image to the Church. A special altar was built in its honor, where the Image is venerated to this day. In 1505, a decorative box was built in Florence to house the Image of Our Lady properly. The money for this casing was donated by the loving people of Bagno. Many more miracles have been attributed to prayers to Our Lady at the Miraculous Image here.

Why, we wonder did our Lord and His Mother perform yet a second miracle here in Bagno di Romagna? Those of us with a devotion to Mary might go back to the Bible, to the Wedding Feast of Cana. The last recorded words of Our Lady in Sacred Scripture are "Do as He tells you". She, being a good Jewish Mother, and very protective of Her Son, may have been saying just that to the people of Bagno. "My Son gave you the very special gift of His Blood in 1412, and you've taken it for granted, ignored it, gone back to your wretched ways. Well, I'm here to confirm that miracle, and to repeat what I said at Cana, Do whatever He tells you." Why not?

Bologna, 1333: Dying of Love

Bologna is a very famous city in Italy, famous for that matter in all Europe. It boasts Europe's oldest University. At one time in the 14th Century there were 10,000 students attending the University of Bologna. During this century, Marconi worked at that University on his wireless, which became the radio. Because the city has always attracted intelligent people, freethinking has been a way of life for inhabitants of Bologna. But freethinking can breed agnosticism and atheism, as well as anarchy and radicalism. Bologna has been known for all of the above. In the 1970's, Bologna was a hotbed of a homegrown breed of terrorists, the Red Brigade, along with Turin, Padua and Milan.

On the other hand, Bologna is the resting place of many saints of the Church, one of which is St. Dominic, the founder of the Dominican Order, and co-reformer with St. Francis of Assisi of the Church of the thirteenth century. Another is St. Catherine of Bologna, whose incorrupt body is seated in a small church. During World War II, the entire church was destroyed, except for the little Chapel which is the Sanctuary of the saint.

There is also, in St. Sigismondo, a little Parish Church near the University, the body of a very special little girl, Blessed Imelda Lambertini named the Protectress of First Holy Communicants by Pope St. Pius X. She was born of a very noble

Bolognese family. Her father was Count Egano Lambertini. From the time she was a small child, she was known for her piety and spirituality. It was obvious that she would devote her life to God. It was not known that it would be such a short life. Imelda was a joy to her parents. She was a pretty little girl, but things of the world had no value for her. She spent much time by herself in prayer in various corners of the house where she would not be distracted.

It was no surprise when she asked her parents for permission at age nine to enter into the religious life. She was placed in the Dominican Convent of Santa Maria Maddalena in Valdipietra. She was loved very much by the nuns in the Convent, as they watched her grow in the spiritual life. Being the youngest in the community, and probably the most loved, Imelda was treated as a very special gift from the Lord. The nuns could tell that this was no ordinary child. She was extremely happy with them, taking to the community life immediately; she was an example to many of the older nuns.

Imelda had an all consuming love for Our Lord Jesus in the Eucharist. She longed to be able to take part in Communion, but at that time she was not yet able to do so because First Communion was delayed until age 12. When the other sisters received the Eucharist at Mass, she yearned to be able to take part in the Eucharistic Feast. She grieved for this one gift of the Lord that was refused her. She was heard to have said "Tell me, can anyone receive Jesus into his heart and not die?"

But the Lord had a special gift for her, a Eucharistic Miracle. It took place on the feast of the Ascension in 1333. The community was at Mass. Blessed Imelda prayed fervently during this particular Mass. When the Mass ended, the sisters proceeded to leave the Church. Imelda stayed behind to continue praying. The sisters turned to call Imelda. What they saw astonished them. A bright white Host appeared above the head of Imelda, and remained suspended in air. They immediately called the priest. Upon witnessing what had happened, the priest took

Blessed Imelda's body is incorrupt. She died in ecstacy after receiving First Holy Communion (Bologna).

a paten, and went to where Imelda was kneeling. The bright Host, still suspended over her head, descended onto the Paten. The priest took this as a sign that Imelda was to be given her First Holy Communion. He administered the Lord to her. She swooned, and went into an ecstasy, from which she never returned. She died that same day. Thus, her first Communion was also to be her last. The date was May 12, 1333. Imelda was 11 years old.

Her story is short. Her life was short. But it was more complete than many people who live to be 100. The Lord had a very definite example He wanted to set by the devotion this young creature had for Him in His Precious Body and Blood. In St. Mark's Gospel, 10:14-15, Jesus tells us: "Let the children come to me and do not hinder them. It is to just such as these that the Kingdom of God belongs. I assure you that whoever does not accept the reign of God like a little child shall not take part in it." The pure faith of this child was so strong that Our Lord Jesus put aside the laws of nature to reward her, and instruct us.

Devotion to this little Blessed person began almost immediately after her death. Many devotional booklets were written about her, especially in connection with the Eucharist. Wherever a great devotion to the Eucharist arose, or heresy denying the Eucharist, prayers for the intercession of Imelda followed. In 1922, a community of Dominicans was instituted, called Dominican Sisters of the Blessed Imelda. Their Charism is to spread the Eucharistic Spirit by means of Perpetual Adoration to the Blessed Sacrament, and to give moral, intellectual and religious aid to young people. This community also does missionary work in Brazil.

Blessed Imelda's body is venerated in the Parish Church of San Sigismondo, near the University in Bologna. It is very fitting that she be there, close to young people. We would like to say that the young people need to take example and inspiration from Blessed Imelda. But that would only be half a truth. People young and old alike need to take inspiration from her.

We have a responsibility to those that follow us, as our ancestors had to us. There is a lot of anger in our young people today, because of the world situation. They consider the Nuclear Age we live in as a vast problem that our generation has gifted them with. We, for our part, put the blame on those who came before us. The same can apply to our spiritual world. There are those who believe that our Church has lost all its tradition, and that our children have nothing to hold onto. What legacy are we giving our children for their souls?

What will our children and grandchildren give as a legacy to those who follow them? Will it be the endtimes? Or will a bright star, such as Blessed Imelda Lambertini, brilliant with the pure love she possessed for Our Lord Jesus, be able to light up the hearts and souls of our generation, and the next, and the next?

Volterra, 1472:
Clearly the Son of God

As you travel through the Italy of today, the Italy of yesterday can be seen on all sides. Looking to the right and to the left, you pass Medieval towns, kingdoms of yesterday, high on hilltops. They were situated in this manner so that the people of the town could see invaders approaching, and defend themselves against the oncoming enemy (which was usually the neighboring city). It's hard to understand, unless you can visualize, say, Brooklyn being invaded by Manhattan, or Los Angeles under attack by Anaheim.

During the Middle Ages, most of the cities in Italy were little city-states. Provinces, like Tuscany, Venice and Milan were small Kingdoms. There was constant backstabbing between the various provinces and cities. The Medicis, the Borgias, the Pittis were all trying to take over smaller areas to build their individual empires. Caught in the middle of these intrigues were little republics like Siena, Lucca, and Pisa, of which Volterra is a part.

This background is necessary to mention in that it was into this, or because of this that we find Our Dear Lord Jesus jeopardized. One of the Medicis, Lorenzo by name, had decided that the small mountain town of Volterra would be a good addition to his Florentine empire. He also thought it would not be too expensive a proposition to take over the town. To this end, he hired a group of mercenaries, headed by the Duke of Urbino, Frederick of Montefeltro.

The nobility of the time put great stock in their honor, although many had little or none. This particular siege was underhanded at best, and without any honor to begin with. To compound the insult, Lorenzo financed his expedition by stealing the dowries of poor girls. Had the mercenaries just done their job, it would have been bad enough. However, mercenaries being what they are, this group decided to pillage and rape.

The disgrace spread itself even to the church of St. Francis in the town of Volterra. One of the mercenaries came into the church in search of loot. He had not done well in the town, and hoped that he would be able to find something of value in the church. He headed immediately for the tabernacle, where we know the most precious "Valuable" in the world lives. His goal was not Our Lord, though, but treasures of the earth.

Inside the tabernacle, he found a box, most likely a pyx. It was made of ivory, and inside was the Blessed Sacrament. Either he was not aware that Our Lord was in the box, or didn't care. In any event, he threw the box into his bag, and started to leave the church. The Franciscans in the church began to pray feverishly. They didn't want the Eucharist to leave the church, especially in the hands of this soldier. But they were afraid to say anything to him, for fear he would kill them.

A strange thing happened. He couldn't find the door of the church. He staggered around several times, cursing and threatening the priests. Then his sight left him completely. He was blind. He flew into a rage. Panic overtook him. He withdrew his sword, swinging it wildly as if to hit some invisible force that had taken over his body. The more helpless he became, the wilder he acted, and the more he cursed.

The priests must have felt the presence of the Lord in their midst. They gathered up courage. They told the soldier that if he would give back the box with the Body of Our Lord Jesus, perhaps his sight would be given back to him. The thief hesitated, cursed some more, then plunged his hand into his bag to feel for the case he had stolen. As he grabbed it, he began to rant and rave, as if he were possessed by Satan. He screamed a blood-curdling scream. His face contorted grotesquely. He flung the box against one of the columns of the Church.

At the instant the box struck the column, the earth began to shake throughout the city. It sounded like a groan from heaven. It was reported as the worst earthquake ever to hit that city. It calls to mind the Gospel account of the events following the Death of Our Dear Lord Jesus. In Matthew 27:51, "Suddenly the curtain of the sanctuary was torn in two from top to bottom. The earth quaked, boulders split, tombs opened. . . . The centurion and his men who were keeping watch over Jesus were terror-stricken at seeing the earthquake and all that was happening, and said 'Clearly this was the Son of God.'"

The thief was completely distraught. Between his blindness and the terrible earthquake, he fell to his knees in tears of sorrow and fear. He confessed all his sins, and asked for forgiveness. The Franciscans prayed with him. The thief regained his sight. The ivory box shattered all over the floor, but the Sacred Host remained intact. The Host was reverently picked up by the priests, and placed back into the tabernacle.

The event, witnessed by one Biagio Lisci, was put into the archives of the church. Another account, confirming the above events, was recorded in 1576 by Ludovico Falconini, chancellor of the Episcopal Curia. He was a well known citizen from a family dating back to the time of this occurrence. The documents are there to this day in Latin. The church has become a Sanctuary of Our Lady. The custodian of the sanctuary is also the keeper of the original texts.

For our purposes, the narrative ends here, only because we have no more solid information, but we wonder how this story really ended. What did the Lord have in mind when He performed this miracle? Was it in anger for the sacrilege committed against His body? Was it to give strength to the people of the town who had been violated so brutally by these invaders? Was it for the soldier? Was this another St. Paul in the making? The story of the soldier, the blindness, the repentance, is such a parallel of St. Paul, one of the strongest soldiers the Lord ever converted to His work. In the Conversion of St. Paul, he was thrown off his horse and blinded. In Volterra, the soldier was blinded. Jesus asked St. Paul "Saul, why do you persecute me?" In Volterra, was this Jesus' way of asking the soldier, "Why do you persecute me?"

A priest was once giving us a teaching about the young man who asked Jesus what he must do to go to heaven. And when Jesus told him to sell all he had, give it to the poor, and come back to follow Jesus, the young man walked away in sorrow. Our priest said, "I would like to think that two years later, the young man came back to Jesus and said 'I've done it. I've given it all up. I'm ready to follow you'."

What happened to the soldier? Did he continue as a mercenary, or was he truly converted? Did he go on to do great things for the Lord for the rest of His life? Why not?

Turin, 1453: Benediction

The history of our Church has been one of turmoil. The sun can be compared to the Host, the Body of Our Lord Jesus in the Eucharist. The gleam of the sun is like the life giving rays of the Eucharist. It nourishes us; It warms us; It gives us life. When It shines on us, we are enveloped in the compassion of His love. The black storm clouds that block out the life and warmth of the sun are the enemies of the Eucharist. From the beginning of the Church, they have tried to prevent the life blood of the Church, the Eucharist, from reaching us. But the Light of the World, Jesus in the gift of the Eucharist, has always managed to break through the cloud cover, and beam down to us. He uses many means to get the job done, people, situations, and very often, miracles.

Every war that has been waged, when analyzed at the root, has been a religious war. The people of God, down through the ages, have been in constant struggle against the powers of darkness. The list of enemies, Caesar, Nero, Attila the Hun, Mohammed II, Napoleon, Hitler, Stalin, Ho Chi Minh, Arafat, Ghaddafi, and whoever is chosen to follow them, reads like a who's who of Evil. Their justifications range from spreading culture through Colonialism, to preserving the Aryan Race, to safeguarding the state against its enemies, to helping the Palestinians regain their country, and on and on. But when we break it down, when we get to the base, it's a war between the two major powers of the world, God and the Devil.

In the year 1453, Mohammed II captured Constantinople, massacring hundreds of thousands of Christians. His plan was to continue his attack of terror throughout Europe. The logical thing for the Europeans would have been to join forces to stop this attack. But the powers of evil, the dark clouds, distracted the powers of the European countries by creating conflicts from within. Italy was a perfect example of this, and one which demanded immediate attention from Jesus.

As we have seen, cities like Milan, Turin, Venice and Florence were not cities at that time. They were little empires, and they were constantly warring with each other. The dukedom of Milan was up for grabs after the death of its ruler, Francesco Maria Visconti in 1447. A weak republic was formed by the people, which was doomed from the outset. In 1450, as a result of infighting, the drowning republic pleaded for help to one Francesco Sforza, a powerful force in Italy. He immediately proclaimed himself Duke of Milan, and the battle began.

The various dukes who had Milan in their sights, the Duke of Venice, the Duke of Naples, the Duke of Monferrato, and the Duke of Piedmonte and Savoy began a war that lasted four years. We can easily see the distraction. During this conflict, Mohammed II had built up forces, attacked and conquered Constantinople, and proceeded northwest. The Italian powers were so involved with the war over Milan, that they didn't pay attention.

Francesco Sforza was not strong enough to resist this enormous barrage against him. His only ally in Italy was Florence, and that was not enough. In desperation, he enlisted the aid of other foreign powers. The Duke of Anjou and Lorraine had eyes on the kingdom of Naples and Sicily. He agreed to help Francesco Sforza in Milan in exchange for Naples and Sicily, after the smoke of the battle had ended.

The army of Anjou and Lorraine marched towards Milan in defense of Sforza. However, they had to pass through Piedmonte, which was ruled by one of the enemies of Milan. The attitude of their leader, Ludwig, was that if they were friends of his enemies, they were his enemies also. So when the army approached Piedmonte, they had to engage in battle with the Piedmontese troops. In a bloody battle, the troops of Anjou were turned back. This took place in the countryside of Exilles, where our miracle took place.

When the Piedmontese troops crossed into the country of Exilles, and the troops from Anjou approached, all the peasants, indeed, everyone living in that area, left their homes. After the battle, the troops from Anjou retreated from the countryside. The Piedmontese soldiers began looting the homes and churches in the villages. One particular soldier entered the local church in Exilles, and forced open the tabernacle door to steal the monstrance. He grabbed it, knowing but not caring that he had also taken the Consecrated Host contained inside, the Body of Christ. The monstrance was used for Benedictions. The soldier threw the monstrance into his sack, and loaded it onto his donkey.

The animal was uncomfortable with the sack on his back, probably because the Lord made it that way. The sack kept falling off the animal's back. The soldier wanted to get rid of his stolen goods anyway, so he sold the entire sack to the first merchant he came across, at what we would call a highly discounted price. That merchant in turn sold the sack to another merchant, who sold it to another merchant. By the time the last merchant bought the sack, he was headed for Turin.

He entered the city with a donkey carrying the sack. At the church of Saint Sylvester, the donkey stumbled and fell. His owner tried to get him up. The animal refused to move. His owner began to beat him. A crowd gathered. No one liked to see animals mistreated. The larger the crowd, the more frustrated the merchant became. He beat the donkey unmercifully.

The donkey moved from side to side, trying to avoid the lashes of his master. The sack slipped from the donkey's back, and fell to the ground, spilling the contents all over the street.

All eyes focused on the monstrance, or rather the Host inside. It glistened, becoming so bright that they had to avert their eyes from the glare. The monstrance rose into the air, to a height of about 10 or 12 feet, at which point It stopped, and remained suspended in the air. The crowd uttered gasps of disbelief at the Miraculous Sign in their midst. From the Church of St. Sylvester, Fr. Coccono noticed the crowd, and came to see what was attracting them. Once he saw the monstrance floating freely in the air, he was aware that this was a sign from the Lord. The priest ran off to inform the Bishop of what was happening.

The Bishop immediately assembled a procession of priests from the Cathedral, and started off towards the Square. Word spread quickly, and officials of the city filed in behind. When the bishop arrived at the scene, the monstrance opened, and fell to the ground, leaving the Sacred Host in suspension. It was surrounded by a dazzling aura. The bishop began chanting a hymn in Latin, joined by the priests. The townspeople sang "Resta con noi," "Stay with us."

The Host began Its descent. The bishop held out a chalice. The Miraculous Host floated down, and gently landed in the chalice. The townspeople marveled at this, and followed the bishop in procession to the Cathedral. The Vatican was immediately advised.

The date of this miracle was June 6, 1453. Eight days before this, Mohammed II conquered Constantinople, and seated himself in the Cathedral of St. Sofia. In the same time period, another Eucharistic Miracle occurred in Langenwiese, a small town between Poland and Czechoslovakia. Shortly after, the war for control of Milan ended.

Veneration of the Eucharistic Miracle of Turin began immediately. Pilgrims from all over Italy and later from all over Europe gathered at the Shrine. In the meantime, word drifted up from the southeast that the Arabs were moving towards

Poland and Czechoslovakia in their effort to destroy Christianity. In 1455, the hierarchy of the church of Turin unanimously voted to have an honorary tabernacle made to conserve the Eucharistic Miracle. The following year, the Arab invasion was stopped at Belgrade.

The tabernacle was completed in 1459. Thirty years later, however, the Cardinal Archbishop of Turin, Domenica della Rovere, gave the order for a new cathedral to be built, and a new tabernacle to house the Eucharistic Miracle. The Host was kept in the new tabernacle until a new marble shrine was erected at the spot where the donkey had fallen in 1453.

The entire city of Turin rallied around the miracle. The city put up a small marker after the miracle had occurred, at the place where the donkey had fallen. It became such a strong place of Pilgrimage that the Pilgrims couldn't be contained in that small area. An actual building was put up in 1521 as a place of devotion for the people. The Oratory was built over the place where the donkey had fallen. In 1525, the Company of Corpus Christi was instituted to be protectors of the Eucharistic Miracle. Their badge was the Monstrance, with the Host suspended in air above. They were put in charge of the marble Oratory built in honor of the miracle and the place where the donkey fell.

A strange thing happened around the year 1584. The exact date is not certain. Word came from the Holy See that the Eucharistic Miracle was to be consumed. This is very unusual. From what we can gather, the Host was still in an incorrupt form. The justification given by the Vatican was ". . . in order not to obligate God to keep this Eucharistic Miracle incorrupt forever." It has been our experience in researching these shrines and miracles, that as long as they were incorrupt, the Eucharistic Miracles were never touched.

It is only due to the Lord that devotion to this beautiful Sacred Host, snatched away from the people, did not stop with the Papal order of 1584. They continued venerating the Eucharistic Miracle. In 1598, in the midst of yet another war, this time between the Piedmontese and the French, a plague broke out over the entire province. As if the deaths due to the bloodshed of the war were not enough, the plague destroyed many others. If the Lord was giving a message to the people, it was picked up immediately by the Town Council of Turin. They made a promise to Jesus; if He would only spare the people from the deadly disease, a brand new church would be built in honor of the Blessed Sacrament of Turin. The Lord agreed; the plague ended.

In 1607, the foundations were laid for the new church, which was finished in 1671. To the left of the main altar, an area closed in by a railing is the spot where the donkey fell. There is a plaque, with an inscription in Latin. St. John Bosco (or as we know him, St. Don Bosco) translated it as follows:

> Here, on the 6th of June, 1453, the donkey fell who
> was carrying the Body of the Lord—
> Here the Sacred Host, loosed from Its bonds, rose
> in the air—
> Here It descended kindly to the supplicating hands
> of the Turinese—
> Here, therefore, remember the miracle, kneel on
> the ground and venerate and fear the sacred place.

In the little church of Exille, where the robbery took place that day in 1453, the broken tabernacle has never been fixed. They kept it in its original form as a tribute to the Miraculous Occurrence.

On the various Centenaries of the Feast, solemn processions and celebrations have taken place. In 1853, St. John Bosco wrote about the feast and the extensive preparations that were made in anticipation for it. That particular feast was highlighted by the presence of Queen Adelaide, wife of Vittorio Emmanuele II, and Queen Maria Teresa, widow of Carlo Alberto, both of whom received Communion in the Basilica. In 1953, the date of the celebration of the 5th Centennial was moved up to September 6 through the 13th, to coincide with the Eucharistic Congress that was held there that year.

Special hymns have been written in honor of the Eucharistic Miracle of Turin. They are sung on the feast days, and especially during the Centenary celebrations. They are as follows:

We sing with due praises
the total power of God
and the greatest pledge of the divine love
towards this city.

Here the animal stopped
burdened with the Precious Weight
Here, from the evil predator
he freed himself of the burden.

It rises into the air
Splendid Divine Host
the truth of the faith triumphs
and heresy is confused.

Turin is a large industrial city. It is also an intellectual city. Over the years, Turin has always been known as a hotbed of insurrection and unrest. There was a reason, a very important reason why the Lord chose Turin to be the recipient of this Eucharistic Miracle. Even Turin's distance from the scene of the battle which precipitated the entire affair is amazing. It probably took place on the French side of the mountains. Even if it had happened on the Italian side, it could only have been Divine Direction that brought the sack, changing hands only the Lord knows how many times, into Turin.

In all our years of travel and research, only once have we been robbed. Our car was broken into outside the Church of the

Holy Shroud in Turin, before we learned of the miracle. Then we were told that the Red Brigade (while they were in existence) had had their headquarters in Turin. We decided that the Turinese were not our kind of people, and that we would never go back to Turin again. The Lord does strange things to people, especially us. A few years after this incident, we were at a Papal audience at St. Peter's Square in Rome. We were waiting for the arrival of His Holiness, Pope John Paul II. As is our custom, we spoke to the people sitting around us. We met a beautiful mother and son, with whom we became very close. You guessed it; they were from Turin. Then we learned about this Eucharistic Miracle. Needless to say, the Lord has brought us back to Turin.

The events leading up to the Eucharistic Miracle in Turin, both on the side of the Lord, and on the side of the devil, give us a concentrated view of how they work in the entire world. Jesus allows Lucifer to wreak his havoc throughout the world, while He counterattacks Satan on every side. For every action on the part of the devil, there is a reaction on the Lord's part, to protect and save us from evil.

Avignon, 1433:
Dividing the Waters

The Sorgue is a small river, running through the city of Avignon, in Southern France. If the name Avignon rings a bell, there is good reason. It is world famous as the Sanctuary of the Popes. It became the home of the Popes from 1309 to 1377.

Towards the end of the Thirteenth Century, many factions within Italy were trying to take over Rome and the Papal States. One family in particular, the Colonna family, was attacking the Popes. In 1304, Pope Benedict XI fled Rome to Perugia, near Assisi, where he died the same year. Pope Clement V, the first Pope of Avignon, was elected in Perugia on June 5, 1305. He was a Frenchman, who accepted the offer of the King of France to rule the Church from France. He had ulterior motives. While it was true that Italy was a battleground, and the Pope one of the main targets, he also wanted to reconcile France and England in order to get them to help him launch a new crusade in the Holy Land. It was not until March of 1309 that he actually took up residence in Avignon.

The first two popes who had residency in Avignon, Clement V and John XXII, considered Avignon as temporary living quarters, and the last two, Urban V and Gregory XI, wanted to return to Rome. Urban V did go back to Rome in 1367, but returned to Avignon in 1370. Gregory XI had made a secret promise to the Lord before he became Pope, to bring the Papacy back to Rome. Only he and Jesus were aware of this promise. So, when Catherine of Siena reminded him of the promise he had made, Pope Gregory XI knew it was the Lord who was speaking to him. He returned to Rome in 1376.

This caused what has been termed the Great Western Schism, in which there was a Pope of Avignon, who was recognized only by France, Spain, and the Kingdom of Sicily, and another Pope, the Roman Pope, successor of St. Peter. This situation lasted until 1409. What remains in Avignon are the Pope's Palaces, which were built during the 67 years of their residence.

There is, however, another event, perhaps more important, which makes Avignon a place of Pilgrimage for us. In order to fully understand the significance, we have to go back 217 years from the time of the miracle, to 1226. The Albigensian heresy, which got its name from the town of Albi, France, was spreading its false teachings throughout the southern part of the country. The heresy condemned all the sacraments, especially marriage. Sexual permissiveness was promoted by the Albigensians. The Eucharist was completely rejected. Albigensianism was condemned by the Church as early as the Eleventh Century, but it wasn't until the Albigensians began serious attacks on the secular governments, that the heads of the countries where they had their greatest stronghold denounced and outlawed them.

The Albigensians were very powerful in 1226, especially in Southern France, where Avignon is located. As a means of combatting their attack on the Physical Presence of Jesus in the Eucharist, King Louis VIII, father of St. Louis IX, had a church built on the banks of the Sorgue in honor of the Blessed Sacrament. He ordered that the Blessed Sacrament be exposed at all times in a monstrance. The church was put under the custodianship of the Gray Penitents, of the Franciscan Order.

The Sorgue River tended to overflow every few years.

When these acts of God occurred, the water came up the banks of the river and flooded homes and farms in the immediate vicinity. A particularly mighty flood came after heavy rains during late November of 1433. The water exploded over the banks, moving farther inland than in previous years. It was one of the worst floods known to the little area.

On the evenings of November 29 and 30 the water level rose to a dangerous peak. The Grey Penitents of the Franciscan Order were sure that the little church that King Louis VIII had built, where the Blessed Sacrament was exposed day and night, was flooded. They decided to go there to save the Consecrated Eucharist and bring It to dry land. Two of the superiors of the Gray Penitents got into a boat, and rowed their way to the church. Keep in mind that when they arrived, the water was halfway up the front door of the church. However, when they opened the door, to their amazement, they found that the entrance from the door to the altar was completely dry. Our Lord Jesus in the form of the Consecrated Host in the Monstrance, stood regally on top of the altar, completely dry.

The water had piled up against the walls. It was reminiscent of the Bible account of the Parting of the Red Sea. Indeed, it appeared that way to the Gray Penitents also. They looked for some other members of the Gray Penitents, who came and verified the miracle. The four Friars prayed in unison, and brought the monstrance, containing the Blessed Sacrament to a Franciscan Church on dry ground. When they had placed the monstrance on the altar, they read from the book of Exodus regarding the Parting of the Red Sea (Exodus 14:21): "Then Moses stretched out his hand over the sea, and the Lord swept the sea with a strong east wind throughout the night, and so turned it into dry land. When the water was thus divided, the Israelites marched into the midst of the sea on dry land, with the water like a wall to their right and to their left." The Franciscans wrote the account of the four Friars into the records of their community, where it is preserved till today.

A tradition was created at that time, which is still in practice. On the 30th of November each year, in the chapel of the church in Avignon, the Gray Penitents put a rope around their necks, and, devoutly crawling on their hands and knees, they recreate the incident, retracing the steps of their predecessors, following the same path that was taken on the evening of the miracle.

There is nothing left but the church, and the tradition of the miracle. But in the tradition, these Friars give thanks to the power of Our Lord Jesus in the Blessed Sacrament, for having given them a sign, no less than that which saved the Jews from the hands of the Egyptians during their Exodus. Pilgrims, especially those with a hunger for the Eucharist, still visit the little Church on the banks of the river, to venerate and give thanks to the Lord for giving us this special gift at a time when we needed His Strength.

What is the significance of this miracle? Why were the symbols of the Exodus of the Jews from Captivity used to bring about the miracle? Nothing is known for sure. Speculation abounds among those who have studied this special situation. Could it be that the Lord was using this sign of the Eucharistic Miracle to free His people from the bondage of sin?

In today's world, we find ourselves captives of another sort, subtler, but deadlier. We're in a world of materialism, consumerism, permissiveness, atheism. Our lives are ruled by a peer pressure, manipulated by movies, magazines, records and television advertising. Drugs, alcohol, abortion, pre-marital sex, disdain for parental guidance, self-centeredness and a host of others are just some of the lessons we're being taught daily. If we don't conform to this way of life, we find ourselves imprisoned by non-acceptance and loneliness.

We do have a weapon, however. The same miracle that the Lord performed in the little church in Avignon is performed for us every day during the Consecration of the Mass. Our Daily Miracle of the Eucharist can free us from any invader.

We have to hold onto that miracle. We can't sit back, and wait for something to happen when we receive the Miracle of the Eucharist. We have to lunge forward, embrace Him, and take Him into our heart. We will find ourselves freed from the slavery of the world, and all its false teachings.

The Eucharistic Miracle of the Sorgue could very well have been another way the Lord used to repeat the promise made to us in Luke 4:18: "He has sent me to bring glad tidings to the poor, to proclaim liberty to captives, recovery of sight to the blind, and release to prisoners, to announce a year of favor from the Lord."

The Eucharistic Miracle that takes place in your church every day is this same message from the Lord.

Blanot, 1331: Body and Blood

In our travels through the small villages of Europe, especially those of France and Italy, we have been amazed to find that many of these quaint little hamlets are complete worlds of their own. There may be as few as 1,000 inhabitants in these little towns, and yet they are completely sufficient unto themselves. They have all their own little shops, as well as a police department, post office, town hall, mayor, and on and on. In the United States, half of these villages would be considered ghost towns. When the highway takes the flow of traffic away from a given road, all the locals pack up their homes and move to a larger city. It's not that way in France and Italy. They maintain the flavor and charm of Old Europe.

Blanot is such a village, tucked away in the heartland of France, in a province called Cote D'Or, (the Gold Coast). It's not listed on the map of France. It probably never has been. And yet, it was important enough for the Lord to pick this unknown place to manifest Himself in a way that would catapult Blanot into fame, on a level with Siena and Bolsena for the next 600 years.

The bright sun that rose on Blanot on Easter morning of 1331 did not warm the countryside. Winter had taken its toll, and spring was long in coming. The members of the congregation who braved the cold to attend the first Mass in Celebration of the Resurrection of Our Lord were making a particular sacrifice. They were snapped out of their early morning sleepiness by the biting gusts of bitter wind. There was not much respite inside the church. Though the stone walls of the building blocked the cutting wind, it did not help with the cold. These early morning worshipers were true Christians. Nothing could stop them from praising their Lord in thanksgiving for the gift of their Redemption.

It was six in the morning. The priest, Hugo de Baulmes, was celebrating the Mass. His demeanor reflected the attitude of his parishioners. He was cold, not quite awake, but gloriously happy to be celebrating the end of Lent and the beginning of Easter. Although it required sacrifice, celebrating the First Mass on Easter Sunday was a great honor, for which the vicar was most appreciative. He led his congregation in songs of praise of Our Lord, chanting "ALLELUIA" many times, after 40 days of not having been able to say that word.

The highlight of this special Easter celebration, as in all celebrations of the Mass, was the reception of the Eucharist. As the priest consecrated the bread and wine, he remembered the past two days, Good Friday and Holy Saturday, when the Church as he knew it, didn't exist. He took Lent very seriously. On Good Friday, when Our Lord Jesus died on the Cross, the Church went into a limbo state, from which it did not come out until this time, early in the morning of the third day.

At Communion time, the congregation knelt at the Altar Rail, anticipating Our Lord Jesus in the Sacred Host. Fr. Hugo began to distribute the Eucharist. One of the communicants, the widow d'Effours, did not get the entire Host into her mouth. She bit down hard, to avoid letting Our Lord Jesus to fall onto the ground. A fragment of the Host broke off, and began plummeting to the floor. The altar server, Thomas Caillot, caught the small Piece on the pall, (PALL: A Linen cloth, about 5 inches square, folded two or three times, highly starched, which was normally placed on top of the chalice. It was also used to place under the chin of communicants, in the event the Host dropped from their mouth) which he used to protect the Eucharist from falling.

Fr. Hugo did not see what had happened. He continued distributing Communion, and was about to return the Ciborium to the Tabernacle, when Thomas brought his attention to the fragment that had fallen onto the Pall. Thomas called out: "Father, Father. Come around to this side. Here, on the Pall, a piece of the Body of Our Lord has fallen from the mouth of this woman."

The priest quickly moved towards the altar server holding the Pall. His intention was to consume the fragment of the Host. As he took the Pall, the Host disappeared, and in its place, a small drop of blood appeared. It did not, however, penetrate the Pall, as is normal with a blood stain. It sat on top of the cloth. It was three dimensional, more of a small mound of blood than a stain.

Fr. Hugo took the blood stained cloth into the Sacristy, and began washing it with lukewarm, pure water. He rubbed it many times, five or six at least. The stain became wider. It did not wash out, though the water that dripped from it into the washbasin was blood red. Finally, when the priest realized the Blood was not about to leave the Pall, he cut off the bloodstained part, and went back into the body of the Church.

All the members of the congregation had witnessed the miracle. They were not about to leave the Church while the Miracle took place. They waited for the drama to unfold. Fr. Hugo brought the bloodstained cloth out from the Sacristy with much reverence. He called for a monstrance to be brought to him. He solemnly placed the Miraculous Pall into the monstrance, and exclaimed to the people: "Good people, you can believe it. This is truly the Blood of Our Lord Jesus Christ. Notwithstanding my having given It a good washing and scrubbing, there was no way of separating It from this Pall."

The priest wept tears of joy, bewilderment and thanksgiving. He had probably labored in the fields of this small parish in the middle of nowhere for most of his priestly life. He was not near the mainstream of activity, the seat of the Diocese. Possibly he had never been given any real words of encouragement in his ministry. Perhaps he even felt ignored by his bishop, or fellow priests. But now, he had been given a gift directly from the Lord, his Master. Was this Jesus' way of saying "good work, my son. I am proud of how you have served me all these years"?

Word of the miracle spread quickly throughout the region. The Bishop of Autun, the nearest Diocesan seat, sent a representative to Blanot on the Sunday after the Fifteenth day of Easter. He brought a retinue of priests and notaries with him to help determine the authenticity of the alleged miracle. Fr. Hugo brought eyewitnesses of the Eucharistic Miracle before the investigating committee. They described the events of the early morning Easter celebration, when the Host had turned into Blood. At the end of the inquiry, the committee sent by the Bishop agreed unanimously that the Lord had visited the people of Blanot in a special way, through the Eucharistic Miracle. Based on their findings, the bishop gave his approval, also.

The following year, Pope John XXII bestowed special indulgences on those who celebrated Mass at the Church of Blanot. He also awarded indulgences to those who would donate vestments in honor of the miracle, and to anyone who followed the Eucharistic Miracle in procession. Pilgrims flocked to Blanot. The blessed pall was placed in a permanent crystal reliquary. Blanot became the focal point of many parish pilgrimages. Banners of the various parishes led the procession of the Eucharist. At times, there were as many as 12 or more parish banners at the head of the pilgrim processions.

The miraculous pall was investigated again in the 18th Century by the Bishop of Autun. He verified that it was still perfectly preserved, that the color of the Blood was rich red, and that the threads of the cloth had not disintegrated over the more than 400 years from the time the miracle had happened.

Prior to the French Revolution, the pilgrimages and processions were stopped by the priests of the parish. Relations between the people and the Church were at a bad state in France. The priests complained that the pilgrimages had become excuses for drunkenness and debauchery, causing more blasphemy than reverence to the memory of the miracle. Animosity grew to its highest point during the Revolution. Peasants invaded the little church of Blanot, and proceeded to wreck it. Some wanted to destroy the reliquary containing the miraculous cloth, but local residents stopped them. Some of the people and a nun hid the Eucharistic Miracle in a private home. It was revered in that place on Sundays and Feast Days, until the threat of the Revolution had ended. It was then returned to the Church.

In 1831, the 500th anniversary of the miracle, solemn festivities took place at the Church of Blanot. A permanent place of veneration was dedicated in the Church for the sacred pall. It is always to be found in that part of the church, year round. Today, more than 650 years after the miracle, the cloth is still in good condition. The blood stains are still visible. During the Feast of Corpus Christi, the miraculous cloth is carried in procession after the Blessed Sacrament.

Zaragoza, 1427: The Infant Jesus

Zaragoza has been a city especially blessed by Our Lord Jesus through His Mother Mary and St. James the Apostle from the earliest days of Our Church. Miraculous events of the most unique kind have been attributed to Zaragoza.

St. James, a close relative of Our Lady, and beloved by her, had left Jerusalem for Spain very soon after the Ascension of Our Lord into heaven. St. James and his disciples worked diligently to bring the faith to the people of Spain. He is the patron saint of Spain, and his major shrine, Santiago de Campostello, has been a major Pilgrimage place throughout the centuries, second only to Jerusalem and Rome.

Our Lord Jesus appeared to Our Lady in Ephesus, where she had gone with St. John the Evangelist, brother of St. James. Our Lord asked her to go with the Angels to see St. James, who was in Zaragoza at the time. She was to tell St. James that Our Lord Jesus wished that he return to Jerusalem to be martyred. The tradition of the shrine, (given by Our Lady in an apparition to Sr. Mary Agreda, as written in "The City of God") tells us that Our Lady was carried on a cloud by the angels to Zaragoza during the night. While they were traveling, the angels built a pillar of marble, and a miniature image of Our Lady.

When Our Lady and the Angels arrived at Zaragoza, St.

James and his disciples were deep in prayer. They saw the bright light of the entourage, and heard the heavenly voices of the Angels, chanting hymns in honor of Our Lord Jesus and His Mother Mary. Our Lady gave the message of Jesus to St. James, and added that before he was to return to Jerusalem, a church was to be built on the site where the apparition took place. The pillar and the image were to be part of the main altar. Special graces and protection would be granted the people of Zaragoza, in exchange for a pure devotion to Our Lord and Our Lady.

After the little church was built, Our Lady left with the Angels. St. James, soon after, began his last journey into Jerusalem to be martyred in the name of Jesus. The people of Zaragoza began immediately to celebrate Mass at the little church built by the Angels, and to venerate Our Lady through the image left there by her and the Angels. Possibly the greatest aspect of this miracle is that the people of Spain were venerating the Mother of God under the title of Our Lady of Pilar for *at least 12 years before she died.* According to the Tradition of Sr. Mary Agreda, Our Lady was living in Ephesus when this happened. She was 54 years old. Also, according to the visions of Sr. Mary, Our Lady died at age 67. So her appearance in Zaragoza would have been 12 or 13 years prior to her Assumption into heaven. This is the only apparition that we've ever heard of that took place prior to her death.

The little church is still there in Zaragoza. It has been built over by a much larger church. The miraculous image of Our Lady is there for the faithful to venerate. The Pillar is still there. They are almost 2,000 years old.

We give you this background to make you aware of how important Zaragoza and the surrounding area is in God's plan. As we write of the Eucharistic Miracle of Zaragoza, we make mention of clusters of holy places specially chosen by the Lord over the years. In Zaragoza, there was the Miracle of Our Lady of Pilar in 40 or 41 a.d., and the Eucharistic Miracle in 1427. Near Zaragoza, there were two other Eucharistic Miracles, one

The Miraculous Miniature of Our Lady of Pilar on her Altar in the Church at Zaragoza.

in Viluena in 1601, and another in Daroca in 1239, which we will tell about later on.

There is another place near Zaragoza where the Lord gave us a special miracle. Zaragoza is at one end of the Pyrenees Mountains. At the other end is a little town in France, called Lourdes. We think we know the significance of Lourdes. But in the context of Eucharistic Miracles, do we know how important the Shrine to Our Lady at Lourdes is? A great deal of the cures that are credited to Lourdes happen during the procession of the Blessed Sacrament (or the Blessing of the Sick). This takes place every afternoon at 3:30 at Lourdes.

We have attended these processions many times over the years. The sick are brought on litters and wheelchairs, from the Grotto of Massabiele up to the front of the Basilica of the Rosary. The very last person to process is Our Lord Jesus in the Blessed Sacrament. He is carried to the front of the Basilica. First, all the sick are blessed, and then the rest of the people. How many times, at the raising of the Monstrance for the Blessing, have we seen a wheelchair here and a litter there being rushed through the crowd to get the patient to the hospital. The pilgrims roar! It's a healing! It's a cure! If that's not a genuine, modern day Eucharistic Miracle, nothing is.

For these reasons, and many that the Lord has not revealed, we can say that Zaragoza, and this area of the world, is highly favored by the Lord and His dear Mother Mary. Because of the importance of this place, it has been a target for enemies of Christ over the centuries. Zaragoza has been under attack by Romans, Arians, and the savage fury of the Arab Moslems, which brings us to the time of the miracle. The Moors, or Arab Moslems as we know them today, have been invaders of Europe from the days when the Romans fell. The Arabs ruled this section of the world for 700 years, and so there was, and is, a strong Arab influence in Spain. At the time of the Eucharistic Miracle in 1427, they were no longer in power in Spain, but they were still living there, barely tolerated by their Christian leaders. There was an extreme hatred by the Arab Moslems living in Zaragoza towards the Christians, because they had unseated them from power.

Against this background, we begin the narrative of one of the most unusual Eucharistic Miracles we have researched. There was a married couple living in the city, whose marriage was very stormy. They argued about most everything. They could find nothing good to say of each other. It was almost as if they lived to torture each other. The wife complained bitterly to her friends about her treatment at the hands of her husband. The friends consoled her, but could offer nothing very constructive in the way of advice.

On one occasion when she was bewailing her outcast state, one of her friends suggested she go to a Moslem sorcerer in the town, who could make a love potion which would make her husband return to the amorous way he treated her when they first married. She hesitated, because of her Catholic upbringing, but not for very long. She was willing to investigate; she was not making any commitments.

When she explained her plight to the Moslem sorcerer, he saw a great opportunity for himself, in being able to desecrate and blaspheme the very heart of Christianity, the Eucharist. He was very cunning and the woman very gullible. So he led her along, saying he was not able to give her what she needed, because he didn't have the proper ingredients to make the potion, but. . . .

She fell each time for his bait, becoming more and more frenzied, until she reached such a high pitch, she was ready to kill for the potion. It was then that he told her if she were to bring him a Consecrated Host from the church, he could make her potion. Fear struck her heart. From her Christian background, she knew that this was not only wrong, but Sacrilege. Whether the sorcerer had gotten her so worked up, or her family situation was that hopeless is not known. We do know, however, that the next day she went to the Church of St. Michael in a deceptive attitude of piety. She went up to the altar to receive Our Lord, then withdrew to a dark corner of the church, as if in prayer, to remove the Host from her mouth. She placed It in a sack, and left for the sorcerer's house.

When she arrived, she opened the bag to find, not the Host, but a perfectly formed, beautiful little live baby. A bright aura surrounded His Body. She was in a state of shock. This was more than she had bargained for. She showed the product of her treachery to the Moslem, who was bewildered. But his hate for Christ was stronger than his fear or confusion. He was still ready to go forward with his plan. He convinced her to take the Baby home, and burn It in a fire. She was then to carry the ashes back to the Moslem, who would make a potion which the wife would mix into her husbands food or wine.

The wife, now obviously devoid of all reason, brought the Baby home. She put It on a fire, tying It to a metal rod, and turning It, as you would barbecue a pig on a spit. The results were not at all what the lady expected. Instead of burning up, the Child became brighter and brighter as It was turned in the fire. When the fire went out, the Baby was not only not dead, but was brilliant in light.

The Lord finally had His way. As she ran through the streets, holding the baby in her arms, great tears streamed down her face, tears of fear and repentance. She begged Our Dear Lord for forgiveness. When she arrived at the sorcerer's house, he was completely overcome by the events. He fell to his knees in fear, and begged forgiveness from the God he had so hated, was so willing to blaspheme. He called to Allah, whom he now believed to be also the God of the Christians. The wife and the sorcerer, their attitudes now completely different than when they plotted the sacrilege, went to the Cathedral in Zaragoza; the wife to confess her sins to a priest; the sorcerer in search of the Vicar General of the Diocese, to ask how he could receive pardon for his terrible sin.

The account of the Miraculous Transformation of the Host to a Baby circulated the town like wildfire. The Archbishop, Don Alonso Arbuello, was made aware of the incident. He was very wary. It sounded incredible, so he formed a committee to investigate this mystery. The fact that a Moslem was involved made him very suspicious. The Baby could have been obtained by many means. It could have been kidnapped from a mother after she had given birth.

With all his doubts, two things stood out as irrefutable proof that this was supernatural intervention. The Baby had been put into a fire, and was not burned. This in itself was miraculous. But another, and possibly more important proof was that the Baby was so illuminated. The Archbishop and the committee could actually see that! They knew that the Lord had been working in their midst. They didn't know exactly what was going on, but they knew that they had to determine that this was truly a Divine act.

The Baby was taken from the home of the unhappy husband and wife and that Saturday, in solemn procession, the Baby was transferred to the Cathedral. There were, in the procession, all of the dignitaries of the city. There was the head of the Cathedral, the head of the Church of Our Lady of Pilar, the clergy of all the Religious Orders in and around Zaragoza, as well as all the secular priests of the area. The heads of the city marched in the procession, all the Nobility, and most of the commoners of the town. In short, just about everybody in town was there. At the very back of the procession, the Archbishop, under a canopy, processed with the Child on a golden plate.

The Child was placed on the altar of San Valero, under heavy guard, but where the entire assemblage of Zaragoza could witness and venerate the miracle from heaven. The Baby was kept there all day Saturday, and on Sunday Morning, the Archbishop celebrated the Votive Mass of the Blessed Sacrament, in honor of the Eucharistic Miracle in their midst. During the Offertory, as the Archbishop offered the gifts of bread and wine to the Lord, the Child, gleaming more brightly than ever before, disappeared, and in Its place, the Consecrated Host reappeared.

The Archbishop knew that there was no need to consecrate this Host. It had been consecrated by a Power far greater than himself. He consecrated the rest of the hosts, and at Communion, he consumed the Miraculous Host.

The results of the miracle were overwhelming. Needless to say the woman was repentant, and went on to live an exemplary life. She and her husband were reconciled, not through witchcraft or black magic, but through Divine intervention.

The Moslem was converted. He changed from a vicious enemy of Christ and all things Christian, to a firm worshiper of Our Lord Jesus, and a staunch defender of all things Christian, in particular things concerning the Presence of Our Lord Jesus in the Eucharist.

We, the people of God, were given a twofold gift—first, a unique miracle in which a consecrated Host became a living, breathing human being and then, at a time chosen by God, turned back into its original form again; second, the brilliant light which covered the Child.

Devotion to the Eucharist became extremely strong. The people of Zaragoza have been known down through the centuries, and are considered to this day defenders of the Eucharist. Artists have been inspired by the magnificent Eucharistic Miracle to paint masterpieces which appear in all the churches of the area.

A question arose as to whether the Real Presence of Jesus is present when, by miracle, a Consecrated Host turns into Flesh, or a Baby, as in the instance of Zaragoza. We go to the teachings of St. Thomas Aquinas for the answer. He states: "Under these new aspects, the Body of Christ remains really present in sacramental form." We can also go to Sacred Scripture for inspiration. In Psalm 77, Verse 15, we read: "You are the God who works wonders, among the people You have made known Your power."

La Viluena, 1601: Tried by Fire

La Viluena (or La Vinuela, as it is sometimes called) is just to the west of Calatayud, which is about 50 miles, south of Zaragoza, in Spain. It is also a short distance, maybe 50 miles from Daroca, the scene of another Eucharistic Miracle. So if you look on a map of Spain, and mark these towns you will see a very definite cluster of holy places.

In the new church of the village, above the main altar a date is inscribed: 1601. This is the year the Eucharistic Miracle of Viluena took place. The event the Lord chose to preface this miracle was the death of one of the local people of the village, Pedro de Goni. On the evening of November 8, funeral services were held at the village church. Friends of Pedro and his wife Juana came to the services to pay their last respects to their friend and neighbor, and also to see who didn't come.

As is typical of small villages, there was no deacon or sacristan to take care of dressing the altar for the service, or ringing the bells. Two of the local altar boys were recruited to do these jobs. They felt very important. They handled their tasks with a great deal of attention to all the details. Funerals and weddings were the only time they were given opportunity to perform any serious duties in the church.

After the funeral service had ended, the priest and all the

mourners filed out of the church to go to their homes. The two boys had to ring the bells in the bell tower high above the church for an appropriate amount of time, until all the townspeople had returned to their homes. When they felt that they had completed their task, they came down from the bell tower. They had to go through the church to leave. It was dark in the church, except for the candle the boys held to guide them to the exit. One of the boys began to scare his more timid companion. He made ghostly sounds. His joking had the desired results. His companion became deathly frightened. The joker then said in a phantomlike voice, "May the dead man come to take you away."

This was all his horrified friend needed. He threw the candle up into the air, and made a beeline for the exit of the church. He didn't stop running until he was inside his house. His friend followed him, running and laughing all the way.

Apparently, neither boy paid any attention to the candle they had left burning in the church. It had landed on top of the altar, causing the altar cloth to catch fire. The flames spread quickly, since the church was made of wood. Within a short time, the entire interior of the church was ablaze.

The whole town went to sleep without knowing what had happened to the Church. At about one or two in the morning, a transient from another village, who was staying at a local hotel, got up to check on his horse. This was not an unusual thing to do at 9 or 10 o'clock at night, but at that hour of the morning, we can safely assume it was the Lord who awakened the man. As he looked around the night sky, his eye caught a bright light some distance away. It looked like a fire, but if it were a fire, he thought, he would surely have heard the alarm calling the townspeople to come and help extinguish it. He looked more closely. It was a fire. He decided that he had better awaken the people. He ran throughout the town, calling for the people to wake up.

The townspeople responded immediately. They poured out of their homes, some in pajamas and bathrobes, others wearing less.

This was not a time to concern themselves with the fashions of their dress. They ran to the church as one man, attempting to extinguish the fire. By the time they got there, however, the choir portion was one large glowing ember. The heat was too severe to get very close. They tried to get to the main altar, but were unable to. The priest was in their midst, executing orders, trying to save the Blessed Sacrament. Finally, some brave men got to the tabernacle, which was closed. They were able to open it, but when they did, it was empty.

The priest tried to make some logic out of this. The tabernacle had been closed. There had been a small silver chest in the tabernacle, inside which was the pyx, containing the precious Body of Our Lord Jesus. But when the men retrieved the tabernacle from the flames, and opened it, neither the chest nor the pyx could be found. Even if the silver chest had burned, there would have to be some liquefied silver inside the tabernacle. But there was nothing. As the priest and the men who had rescued the tabernacle stood over it, looking perplexed, another man called out to them from a distance of 15 or 20 feet away. His voice shook; he sounded rattled. They turned towards the direction of the voice. They all looked in awe at the sight.

There was a small mound of embers, about 3 feet high, on the top of which sat the silver chest, perfectly intact. Even the veil which covered the chest was not burned. On the top of the veil there were three small sparks, which gave off the appearance of three little stars. The priest opened the chest, to find the pyx inside, perfectly preserved. There were not even scorch marks. The pyx contained six small Consecrated Hosts, and one large Host. They were in perfect condition. They had not yellowed, or turned brown. They were bright white.

After the initial rush of turmoil had subsided, many of the townspeople gathered around the priest and the Blessed Sacrament. They spoke of other miraculous occurrences that night. Those who walked on the fire, or on hot embers were not burned, neither their feet nor their clothes. Others, sick people, said they had ex-

perienced healings. They could actually feel their illnesses leaving them. As the priest and the townspeople listened to these accounts, and realized that the Blessed Sacrament had been removed from a locked Tabernacle and moved some 20 feet from the altar, they knew that there had been Divine Intervention.

The sacred vessel and the Blessed Sacrament were taken from the burned out church, and placed in a safe place. The priest immediately contacted the Bishop of Tarazona, and advised him of the Eucharistic Miracle. He sent a message back to the priest to keep the chest and the Hosts locked up until he could visit the town on one of his pastoral visits. The people of the town excitedly awaited the bishop's arrival. They were sure he would authenticate it as a miracle. They waited . . . and waited. The bishop did not get around to visiting the town for *seven years*. But the enthusiasm and fervor of the little town did not diminish over the years. This was probably also part of the Lord's plan. He tested His people. "What is more important, that I honored you with this miracle, or the recognition from a man, even though he is a bishop? Does it become less of a miracle if this man doesn't acknowledge it, or give it the importance it should have?"

Finally, after seven long years of waiting, the bishop came to the little village of Viluena. The town prepared for his arrival. Everybody dressed in their best clothes. The streets were cleaned. The new church was spotless. All the villagers were present as the bishop opened the pyx. He held up to the assemblage the Hosts, which were still a bright white. But during his investigation, he saw what he *thought* to be the beginning of a change in the chemical structure of the Hosts. They looked, in his opinion, as if they were turning color slightly. He thought it would be a good idea for the miraculous hosts to be consumed. They celebrated a Mass, at which time the Eucharistic Miracle was consumed. It was gone.

The people of Viluena, as well as the priest, were distraught. Why had they insisted that the bishop come? Who needed him? Why did he have to wait seven years before making his visit? What do they do now? The pyx and the chest, both part of the miracle, were kept inside the Tabernacle, as remembrances of the heavenly visit. A column was erected on the spot where the chest was found amidst the great fire that night, seven years before, in memory of the great miracle.

Some years later, new bishops of Tarazona granted special indulgences for adoration of the Eucharist in the Church of Viluena. A Confraternity of the Blessed Sacrament was instituted. On the feast day of the miracle, November 9, there is a celebration in Viluena of the miraculous occurrence.

It's sad that the miraculous hosts were consumed, taken away from the people forever. But that did not diminish the miracle in any way. The fact that we can't see It anymore doesn't mean the miracle never happened. The power of Our Lord was manifested on that night of November 9, 1601. The Blessed Sacrament was miraculously removed from a burning Tabernacle and placed for the entire community to see, on top of a mound of embers. The Blessed Sacrament was not burned. It remained incorrupt. Townspeople who were trying to put the fire out walked on the fire without being burned, nor were their clothes even singed. Sick people experienced healings at the site of the fire.

The miracle occurred. For whatever reason, Jesus allowed It to leave us. Perhaps it was so that the people of Viluena would never forget what He did there, and never take for granted the gift that was given there. For the people of the town who were alive in 1601, there must have been a yearning and a hunger for the miraculous form of Jesus taken from their midst. For the generations that followed, there must have been a pride in the gift their ancestors had received from the Lord, and also a great desire to have been alive during the time of the miracle. But the pride in what had been given the town was so great that they kept the feast alive every year, to this day.

Do we take for granted the Miracle of the Eucharist, performed on the altars of our churches every moment of every day? How would we feel if Jesus removed Himself from our presence? It has happened before in history. There are areas even here in the United States where the Eucharist is not available every day. Let us pray that this precious gift is never taken away from us. Let us adore Him in the Eucharist for as long as He gives Himself to us.

Daroca, 1239: Bleeding Hosts

Daroca is one of the oldest cities in Spain. It is protected by walls on all sides, as well as over a hundred towers. The towers were used to position soldiers in times of battle. This city is located about 50 miles from Zaragoza. It was chosen by Our Lord Jesus, not to be the site of a Eucharistic Miracle, but to be the home of a Eucharistic Miracle. Against great odds and much opposition, the Lord chose this place, and would have His way.

There was a great battle being waged at the end of 1238, and the beginning of 1239, between the Spanish and their dreaded invaders, the Moors. Valencia had already fallen to the Moslems, but a group of armies from the area of the Aragon had joined forces to take control of this kingdom back from their hated enemies.

The Spaniards had their camp on the outskirts of a village called Luchente, and were preparing to capture the castle of Chio in Luchente. There were six commanders present, Don Ximenes Perez, Don Fernando Sanchez, Don Pedro, Don Raimondo, Don Guillermo, and Don Simone Carroz. They also had their priest present, Fr. Mateo Martinez, from the Church of St. Christopher in Daroca. As was the custom of the time, the commanders went to Confession and attended a Mass performed at the camp. After the Consecration, but before the commanders were able to receive

Our Lord Jesus in the Eucharist, word came to them that the Moors had launched a sneak attack. The commanders returned to the field of battle immediately. the priest wrapped the Consecrated Hosts in the corporal, and hid them under a rock some 10 yards away.

The Spaniards were victorious in the battle against the Moors. They took many of the enemy prisoner. When the commanders returned to the camp, they were exhilarated. They asked the priest to give them Communion in thanksgiving to the Lord for the victory over the infidels. Fr. Mateo ran to the spot where the Hosts had been buried. He took the corporal from under the rock, and unfolded it. He gasped at the sight before his eyes. The Hosts had begun to bleed. They stuck to the corporal, making spots of blood appear on the cloth.

The commanders rejoiced at the sight. They took this as a sign from Jesus that they were to be victorious. They had the priest raise the blood stained corporal on a standard, as a banner. They marched back into battle against the Moors, and the castle of Chio was recaptured. Credit for the triumphant battle was given to the Eucharistic Miracle that the Lord had graciously bestowed on them.

Now the problem began. The six commanders were all from various regions of Spain. Each of them believed the sacred corporal should go to his own town, to be revered in the Cathedral. What began as a discussion as to the disposition of the corporal became an argument. They put the question to a draw. In three different draws, the city of Daroca was chosen to be the home of the Eucharistic Miracle. But two of the commanders, from Teruel and Calatayud, disagreed with the procedure of the draw, and its results. They seemed to be in a deadlock. The head general Berenguer of Entenza proposed a compromise solution. They would place the corporal on the back of a Moorish mule, taken in conquest. The mule had never set foot on Christian soil prior to the Arab attack on Spain. The plan was to let the mule wander as he willed, until he found a place to stop. Wherever

The Miraculous Corporal of Daroca clearly reveals drops of Our Lord's Blood.

he stopped was where the Lord wanted the corporal to remain. The plan was put into effect.

The date was February 24, 1239. The mule left the hill of Codol, and began his journey. He was followed in close attendance by priests with lit candles, and soldiers. The first road the mule took was towards Valencia, but he never entered that city. He continued on, crossing a ravine that goes from Catarroja to Manizes, touching Segorbe, Jerica and Teruel. But he did not enter any of those cities. The mule traveled for 12 days, and a distance of over 200 miles before he stopped in front of the hospital of Saint Mark, in the city of Daroca. At that point, he dropped to the ground in a faint. The date was March 7, the future feast day of St. Thomas Aquinas, great defender of the Eucharist. (At the time of the miracle, 1239, St. Thomas was 14 years old. He was later named protector of the Eucharistic Miracle of Daroca after his death, in the middle of the fourteenth century.)

There are traditions or legends attached to the mule's trip, which many consider embellishments. It is said that during the 12 days many miraculous things happened, like angelic music and singing, fury of demons abandoning possessed souls as the mule with the Eucharistic Miracle passed by, many conversions of sinners. But there is no documentation of this. These are local stories which have developed over the years. *There is, however, documentation on the Eucharistic Miracle of Luchente, the pilgrimage of the mule, and the heavenly choice of Daroca as the chosen city for the corporal to be venerated.*

A beautiful Church was built to be the home of this special gift to the people of Daroca. A majestic reliquary was created in 1385. Sculptures depicting the events leading up to the miracle, i.e., the Battle of Luchente, Fr. Don Martinez raising the corporal as a battle banner, the trip of the mule, and the arrival in Daroca, were also placed in the church.

A contingent from Daroca went to Rome in 1261 to inform Pope Urban IV of the Eucharistic Miracle of Daroca.

Pope Urban IV, born James Pantaleon, was a contemporary of Blessed Juliana of Liege, the nun who spent her life trying to institute a feast day for the Blessed Sacrament. Pope Urban IV was the pope who declared the Eucharistic Miracle of Bolsena authentic, and a year later, instituted the Feast of Corpus Christi. It is believed that Pope Urban IV accepted the news of the Eucharistic Miracle of Daroca as one more sign from the Lord that He wanted this feast day instituted.

In 1444, Pope Eugene IV granted a year of Jubilee for Daroca every 10 years. This was the same pope who authenticated the Eucharistic Miracle of Walldurn, Germany, and the Eucharistic Miracle of Ferrara, Italy. It was at this time that the town took St. Thomas Aquinas to be the Protector of the Eucharistic Miracle. Pope Sixtus IV also granted a Jubilee to the Miracle of Daroca, but changed it to occur every 6 years.

The blood on the corporal has been analyzed, and has been determined to be of human origin. There is no data as to the blood type.

Cebrero, 1300: Faith and Doubt

Santiago de Compostela is one of the holiest pilgrimage places in the world. During the Middle Ages, the Road to Compostela was called the Milky Way because of the multitude of lit candles that could be seen along the way to the Shrine. At one time, it was second only to Rome and Jerusalem as an important place of pilgrimage.

The name comes from St. James the Apostle (Santiago in Spanish), the brother of St. John the Beloved, and one of the favored few of Jesus during His ministry. There is no historic proof that St. James came to Spain after the Ascension of Jesus. There is likewise no proof that St. Jude evangelized around the area of Nice, in France. However, there is also no proof that St. James did not come to Spain, and there is an enormous amount of Tradition, including the visions of Our Lady to Sr. Mary Agreda, that St. James came to this country. We also know from the Gospel that Jesus told His Apostles and Disciples to "teach all nations". Sts. Peter and Paul went to Greece, and Rome. St. Jude may have gone to France.

Although it is agreed that St. James died a martyr's death in Jerusalem, tradition has it that his bones were taken by his faithful followers to this land of Spain, which he had come to love. They were put to rest in the northwestern part of the country, in the province of Galicia, in a town named in his honor, St. James of Compostela. Nothing was really known about this place until the middle of the 9th Century, when the tomb of the Saint was discovered. From that time on, the pilgrims commenced in great numbers to venerate the holy city of Santiago de Compostela.

Most of the travel was done through the mountains. There were many roads to Santiago de Compostela. The particular road we are involved with in this Eucharistic Miracle was named the "French Road" or the "Hard Road", because of the difficult mountain passage. When the pilgrims completed this arduous mountain journey, they stopped at the village of Cebrero for rest and recuperation. A monastery and hospice was built to accommodate the pilgrims. At first it was placed in the custodianship of the Benedictine monks, but at the end of the eleventh century, King Alfonso VI entrusted the monastery to the French monks of Saint-Geraud d'Aurillac. At the end of the fifteenth century, 1496 to be exact, the monks of San Benito el Real of Valladolid took over. But at the time of the miracle, the French monks were in charge.

In the year 1300, Our Lord chose Juan Santin, a peasant from Barjamayor, a village near Cebrero, to be the catalyst for this Eucharistic gift. Juan had a great devotion to the Mass, and to Our Lord Jesus in the Eucharist. He attended Mass as often as he could. He let nothing interfere with his attendance at Mass. On the other side of the coin, there was a priest at the church in Cebrero, a chaplain, whose main job was to greet pilgrims as they finished their journey across the mountains. He was a bitter man, who had lost faith in many things: himself, people, and most importantly, his vocation. He went through the motions of the priesthood, but he became withdrawn from the pilgrims, then from his fellow priests, and at this point in time, was withdrawing from Our Lord Jesus. Or so he thought.

We must get into our imaginary helicopter, and fly way up into the sky to see the happenings of that day from God's vantage point. Outside the weather was brutal. Icy cold winds bristled across the mountains, carrying with them gusts of snow. The streets and houses of the little village were so covered with white powder that there was no way to distinguish where one left off and the other began. There was not a footprint in the snow. It was too cold and too windy for man or beast to venture out into the weather. But off in the distance, a miniscule black spot could be distinguished in the blizzard. The dot moved slowly across the snow, towards the town. It got larger as it got closer. It was Juan Santin, heading for the church.

Inside the church was the priest who had lost his faith. He was beginning the Mass. He mumbled and cursed to himself how ridiculous it was to celebrate a Mass in this ungodly weather, when no one would hazard the storm. However, it was his turn to say the early Mass on this blistery day, and so he began. From our helicopter view up above, we can see the progress of the Mass and the progress of Juan Santin. Juan approached the steps of the church as the priest began the Consecration of the Mass.

The doors of the church opened. The wind peeled through the Church, ricocheting off all the walls. The candles on the altar and around the church flickered. Some of the votive candles went out. The candles on the altar just managed to survive the wind. The priest, who had raised the paten with the bread, and the chalice with the wine in Consecration, looked with anger and amazement at the intruder who had caused such a stir in the church. Is this man crazy? the priest thought to himself. How could he brave this kind of weather to come to Mass? And for what? To see a little bread and wine? Did this stupid peasant really believe that a change goes on here? How stupid.

Juan, for his part, upon entering the Church, and seeing His Lord held high before him in the Consecrated Body and Blood, feu to his knees in adoration. This is the contrast we can't help but noticing from our vantage point high above the church in our helicopter. We see the simple, beautiful believer on the one end of the

Church, adoring the God being held in the hands of the disbeliever, whom the Lord had given the power to summon Him from heaven. This is the dramatic scene Jesus set for the execution of the miracle of the Eucharist.

The Host turned into Flesh and the Wine into Blood, before the eyes of the priest, and this beautifully dedicated peasant. Juan was exhilarated at the gift he had been given by His Faithful God. The priest broke down into tears of joy and sorrow at the same time. He knew this gift was for him. He was joyous that Jesus loved him so much that He was willing to upset the laws of nature to prove how important His priests were to Him. The priest was also sorrowful that this was the only way that Jesus could get through to him. He had blocked himself off from all the graces the priesthood afforded him.

We have no more information about the two men the Lord used to accomplish this extraordinary miracle. They were brought together at a moment in time, in a dramatic encounter, and then disappeared, as far as we can tell. We would like to believe that the priest was completely renewed in his vocation, and his devotion to the Body and Blood of Our Lord Jesus. The rest of his life was most likely very pious, and very exemplary. The peasant was given a gift from the Lord that very few experience. He was rewarded in this life for his love and devotion to Jesus in the Blessed Sacrament. He probably became more powerful in his reverence for the Sacraments of the Church, in particular, the Sacrifice of the Mass, and the Holy Eucharist.

The village, which had previously been a stop of necessity because of the long mountain trip, now became a place of pilgrimage on its own. Pilgrimage itineraries were re-routed, sometimes taking days longer to arrive at Santiago, in order for the faithful to be able to venerate the Eucharistic Miracle on the Camino de Santiago de Compostela, as Cebrero came to be known.

Many miracles have been authenticated at this place. One miracle is the manner in which the Host turned Flesh and Wine turned Blood were preserved. The monks left the Flesh on the original paten, and the Blood in the original Chalice for almost 200 years, until the end of the fifteenth century when Queen Isabella of Aragon came on Pilgrimage to Cebrero. She asked to see the Eucharistic Miracle. When It was shown to her, she was not happy with the reliquaries being used to venerate the precious Flesh and Blood. She had two crystal vessels made, one for the Flesh, and the other for the Blood. These are used to this day to contain the Eucharistic Miracle.

A local tradition has emerged over the centuries regarding a statue of Our Lady, which has been in the church since before the time of the miracle. It is said that at the instant the Host turned into Flesh and the wine into Blood, the arms of the statue stretched out and Our Lady inclined her head in honor to her Son, who had caused this miracle to take place. She came to be called "The Virgin of the Holy Miracle", and has been an integral part of the celebrations of the miracle from that time on.

Pope Innocent VIII wrote a Papal Bull in support of the Eucharistic Miracle at Cebrero, authenticating the events of that cold day in 1300. September 9th has been designated as the feast day in honor of the sacred event. On special feast days, such as the Feast of Corpus Christi, the Assumption of Our Lady, and the Birthday of Our Lady, the Flesh and Blood, the original paten and chalice, and the Statue of Our Lady were taken out in procession through the town. Crowds of pilgrims, in the thousands and tens of thousands, ran up the mountain to the village of Cebrero as part of the feasts. Today, the Eucharistic Miracle is only exposed during the special feasts mentioned above. However, as is the case with most of the Eucharistic Miracles in Europe, when a group of pilgrims come to the church, the priest puts on his vestments, lights the proper altar candles, and takes the crystal vessels out to show the faithful.

We sometimes wonder how people who have been living in villages blessed with Eucharistic Miracles, apparitions by Our Lady, and saints having lived there, are able to lose their faith, or their excitement in their faith. How can they become hardened after witnessing the thousands of pilgrims, eyes and spirits aglow, coming year after year to their town, in search of the miracles that are right under their noses? The devil and his forces are constantly at work, and what better place to attack than the places of the shrines. We have witnessed complacency, apathy, and anger at some of the holiest places.

One lesson the Lord consistently tries to teach us is not to take Him for granted. The greatest assaults are on solid members of the Church. Going to church every Sunday, or every day, for that matter, is not enough. When we receive Our Lord Jesus in the Eucharist, are we really aware of what we are eating? Do we consciously believe that Jesus has come down from heaven, and physically enters into us in the Host and the Chalice?

Santarem, 1200's:
Light in the Darkness

There is a concept of God the pilot flying way above the Earth. From His vantage point, He can see great distances, and occurrences that are about to happen and have already happened. Aboard His plane, we can see a pattern that the Lord has created. We see clusters of holy places and events that seem to have no connection with others, except that they were all instituted by the Lord. The chronological sequence may be centuries apart. But time is a limitation put on us by man, not by God. In Yugoslavia, Medjugorje (where the Blessed Mother has reportedly been appearing since 1981) is not that distant from Tersatto, where the Holy House of Nazareth rested before it was moved across the Adriatic to Loreto, Italy.

In Italy, San Giovanni Rotondo, where Padre Pio lived for the first half of the 20th century, is only twenty miles away from Monte St. Angelo, where the Archangel Michael appeared towards the end of the 4th Century.

Portugal is also a place of clusters. It has always been a very special place in the hearts of Our Lord Jesus and His Mother Mary. It has been consecrated to Our Blessed Mother for many centuries. In Fatima, she gave us the message of penance and prayer in 1917. In Batalha, about twenty miles from Fatima, a promise was made to Our Lady to build a great Church in her honor if she would help the Portuguese people in a battle against Spain, which took place on the day before the Feast of the Assumption in 1385. In Alcobaca, in a cluster with Fatima and Batalha, there is a monastery which was built in thanksgiving to Our Lady for enabling the Portuguese to recapture the city of Santarem from the Moors in 1152.

Santarem is also a part of the cluster. It is located halfway between Fatima and Lisbon. The history of Santarem is laced with holy people. For our purposes, however, we will talk of only one important aspect of Santarem.

Sometime between 1225 or 1247 there was a woman living in Santarem, who was very unhappy. She was convinced that her husband did not love her, and was unfaithful. She tried all the wiles known to women from the days of Eve, but to no avail. As a desperate last attempt, she went to a sorceress. The sorceress promised the wife that her husband would return to his loving ways, if the wife would bring her a Consecrated Host.

This greatly frightened the woman. She knew it was sacrilege. She was also convinced that the sorceress was up to no good. The wife didn't know what to do. She finally gave in. She went to Mass at the Church of St. Steven, and received Communion, but did not consume the Host. Instead, she left the Church immediately, and took the Host out of her mouth, putting It into a kerchief. She then headed for the Sorceress.

Along the way, the Host began to bleed inside the kerchief. The wife was not aware of it until passersby brought it to her attention, thinking she was bleeding. Panic struck the heart of the woman. She went home, and put the kerchief and the Host in the bottom of a trunk. She waited all day and into night in fear. When her husband came home late that night, she was sitting in the dark. They went to bed. We doubt whether she slept very much. The guilt of her sin plagued her. She also didn't know if the Host had continued to bleed.

Sometime during the night, they were awakened by bright rays of light coming from the trunk, which lit up the entire room. The wife confessed her sin to her husband. The two of them spent the rest of the night on their knees in adoration before the Miraculous Host. The next day, people came to the house, attracted by the light. They witnessed the miracle for themselves. The parish priest was told. He came to the house, and heard the story from the woman. He brought the Host back to the Church in solemn procession. Encasing It in a wax container, he placed the Host into the tabernacle.

Another miracle occurred. The next time the priest opened the tabernacle door, the wax container had broken into thousands of pieces. In its place was a crystal container with the blood of the Host inside. It has been kept in that church until today. The Church has been renamed, "The Church of the Miracle". The little house where the miracle occurred was on Via delle Stuoie in Santarem. From the time of the miracle until now, every year, on the Second Sunday of April, the incident is re-enacted by local actors. The actual Eucharistic Miracle is processed from the house, which was converted into a Chapel in 1684, to the Church.

The Eucharistic Miracle of Santarem only left the city one time, during the invasion of Portugal by Napoleon's troops in 1810. The people of the town were afraid of desecration at the hands of the French, and so it was taken out of the city. It wound up in the hands of the Bishop of Lisbon, who put It on display for the faithful of Lisbon to venerate. It seemed as if he were going to keep Our Lord Jesus in the church of Pacao permanently. The citizens of Santarem were outraged, and put up a mass protest. It is possible that the Lord did not want the people of Santarem to take His Presence in their midst for granted for even a minute.

The Eucharistic Miracle was sent back to Santarem in great secrecy, to prevent the people of Lisbon from knowing It was leaving their city. The people of Lisbon were not aware that the Physical Presence of their Savior was gone from their

The Sacred Blood of Santarem is preserved in this Miraculous Vial.

city until the day It was restored to Santarem, on December 2, 1811.

The Eucharistic Miracle of Santarem is not normally exposed. However, pilgrim groups with their own priest can usually behold and venerate the Sacred Blood. The Blood is still in liquid form, 750 years after the miracle occurred.

We ask ourselves why the Lord does the things He does? Why was there a miracle in Santarem? Why has it lasted all these years? Why does the Lord form clusters the way we've described? The same question might be asked, "Why does God continue to love us when we are so unfaithful to Him?"

The only answer we can think of is God, to remain God, must love us, because God is Love. God remains faithful because God is faithful. We can turn our back on Him, but He is always there, waiting, arms outstretched, just as when He was on the cross. When we sin, we change. He remains unchanged. When we go to Confession, and are reconciled with Him, the change comes about in us, not in Him. He loves us as intensely as he did before we sinned.

Bois Seigneur Isaac, 1405: Our Lord in Need

The Lord works in mysterious ways. He loves us because He loves us, not because of anything we do. The people He chooses to do His work, or to whom He manifests Himself, often seem to us to be strange choices.

St. Bernadette said, when asked why she was chosen by Our Lady for the Apparitions at Lourdes: "Because I am the lowest of the low." At another time, she said: "The Virgin Mary picked me up like a pebble . . . she used me like a broom. What does one do with a broom when one has finished sweeping? One puts it in its place, behind the door."

There is a small village in Belgium called Ittre, some 15 miles to the south of Brussels. It's not on the map. It's definitely not part of the Tourist Circle. In the year 1405, Our Lord chose this place to give us the extraordinary gift of Himself in a Eucharistic Miracle.

The young man on whom Our Lord decided to bestow the gift of Himself in the Eucharistic Miracle of Bois-Seigneur-Isaac (The Woods of Lord Isaac) was Jean du Bois (John of the Woods). He was a young aristocrat and heir of Lord Isaac. His life was taken up with many things: mostly girls, parties, horseback riding, and various revelries that young men of nobility, not having to work for a living, get involved in. Today we would categorize him as a playboy. This is definitely not the kind of timber you would expect Our Lord to use to be the recipient of a miracle of this magnitude. He possessed none of the virtues that we, using our human logic, would think necessary to qualify him for this great gift. His only saving grace was that we can detect some of St. Francis of Assisi in this John of the Woods. He had inherited a spirituality, still dormant at this time, from one of his ancestors, namely Lord Isaac, who had had a special relationship with Our Lady.

Lord Isaac had built a chapel in honor of Our Lady on his property in the 11th century. A statue of Our Lady was placed in the chapel, under the title "Our Lady of Grace and Consolation". The chapel became a Marian shrine for many of the local people. Miracles and cures were attributed to the intercession of Our Lady at this shrine. Then, in 1336, a devastating plague broke out, which prompted the people to remove Our Lady's statue from the Chapel. They processed with the statue out to the country, petitioning Our Lady to intercede on their behalf to our merciful Lord for an end to the plague. Although their prayers were answered, and the plague was ended, the statue was not returned to the Chapel. For the next 69 years, the chapel was not used as a shrine, until the Eucharistic Miracle took place.

Lord Isaac's descendant John du Bois was not a bad person. He practised the religion of his family, which was Catholic. But like many others, nobility in particular, he was Catholic in name only. Matters of the spirit and the Faith were the farthest thing from his mind. The time of the year was Spring. John didn't need an excuse for distraction from religious things, but Spring would have been a perfect excuse for his thinking about matters of the heart. On the Tuesday before Pentecost, he was sleeping soundly in his bed. It was somewhere around the middle of the night. We can't speculate about what he might have been dreaming, but it's seems safe to assume it had nothing to do with preparing him for what was about to happen. A soft, strong voice called him out of his sleep. As he opened his drowsy eyes, he could see before him a young man, about 30 years old, dressed in a blue coat lined with ermine. A bright aura surrounded the young man. His face was sad. His eyes penetrated John, causing him to awaken quickly. John was startled by the man, the aura, and his unexplainable appearance in John's bedroom.

John asked him what he wanted. Before answering, the young man opened His coat. His body was covered with welts, bruises, and open bleeding cuts. John wanted to turn away, but he couldn't take his eyes off the pitiful sight of the man's body. He had taken a brutal beating. The young man's eyes pierced John's again. Finally, He spoke:

"Look how they have mistreated me. Find me a doctor, and an administrator of justice, someone who will defend my cause."

John was stunned, bewildered. His mind was not functioning. He found it difficult to understand the deep sorrow he felt as he looked at the young man's brutally beaten body. He stammered, apologizing that there was no doctor available to come to his house this late at night. As for finding a judge, or someone in the Government to help bring the evil-doers to justice, John couldn't help but recall all the times he had bragged to people about how influential he was with people in high positions. At this moment, however, the truth of his position was forced on his lips. He didn't know how he could help his uninvited guest receive justice.

The young man showed no signs of disappointment. He continued speaking as if John had said nothing.

"You could find the doctor very easily, if you knew where to look for him." He went on. "How can I not be covered with wounds? They inflict new ones on me every day." The young man then opened his coat wide, and pointed to the largest open wound, in his side, under the heart. "This one," he said, "gives me the cruelest torment."

John du Bois was speechless. He continued to stare at the man standing before him. The young man closed his coat. "If you can't find me some remedy, at least place your hands on my wounds to relieve me. Do what you can. I will be grateful to you until you can do better . . . and I have pardoned the world." With this, he disappeared.

There's nothing to indicate that John touched the Young Man's wounds. We don't know that he spoke to anyone about it the next day. The only thing we know for sure is that John went to bed again the next evening, and that he was visited by the young man again.

The young man appeared to John much the same way as He had the previous night. He showed John his wounds again. He expressed disappointment with John for having done nothing to help heal his wounds. He also said to him, "Must I then get angry against a world that remains deaf to my laments?" John did not respond. It's possible that he really didn't know who was visiting him, and what he was trying to tell him.

The next day, however, he began to react. He shared the experience with members of his family. Their reaction was predictable. Most of them brushed his story off with comments to the effect that he had been partying too much, or had eaten something which didn't agree with him. They didn't believe a word he was saying. His own convictions were not very strong. But he could not get the picture of the young man with all those wounds out of his mind. The vision haunted him throughout that day. He asked his brother to sleep in his room that night. He needed some corroboration. Was this really happening to him or was he a victim of his own mind?

That night, the young man appeared to John again. This time, John, encouraged by his brother's presence in the room, spoke bravely to the Vision. "If I were to call a doctor for you, where would I send him? I don't know who you are, or where you live." At last, the young man knew that he was reaching John. He answered John, "Take the key to the chapel, and go in. You'll find me there, and you'll know who I am."

Then, a strange thing happened. John found himself in ecstasy. Today, we'd call it an "Out of Body Experience". He saw himself leave his body. He was transported by heavenly powers to the chapel. His attention was focussed on the Crucifix of the Savior at the upper part of the altar, which showed Our Lord Jesus covered with open wounds, the greatest being that in His side, under His heart. The Image was almost exactly like that of the Young Man who had visited him three times. Finally, he understood that it was Our Lord Jesus who had come to him. His heart was filled with the spirit of the Lord. It's as if the doors of his mind were opened, and he could understand all that the Lord was trying to tell him.

The ecstasy ended. He was back in his own bed. His heart pounded furiously. He turned to ask his brother what he had seen. The brother was fast asleep. John had not been able to share with his brother any of the things that had happened to him. He woke his brother and, after scolding him for not having been awake to protect him, John shared what had happened. The tables were now turned on John. He found himself in the position of the young man, trying to explain to his brother, who was half asleep, and unable to understand anything John was saying to him.

John burned with excitement the rest of the night. He couldn't sleep. He wasn't quite sure what he would do the next day, but he knew he would be doing something. He was completely committed to the Lord in whatever He wanted of John. He was converted. He was filled with the Holy Spirit.

When the Lord decides to move, the earth moves, and everyone on it. Things begin to take shape. All the pieces fit into place. The local parish priest, Peter Ost, had an Inner Locution (an inner voice) during the night. A heavenly voice told him "Peter, go to the chapel in the Bois Seigneur Isaac tomorrow morning, and celebrate the Mass of the Holy Cross." He was not required to celebrate Mass in the morning, because he was scheduled to celebrate an anniversary Mass at his own church in the evening. In addition, he had celebrated Mass at the chapel three days before. So this was not a normal thing for him to do. But Peter Ost was a man of faith and obedience. It was not important that he didn't understand what it was all about. He felt the Lord speaking to him, and he obeyed.

He got up early in the morning, and began the trip across the woods to the Chapel of Bois Seigneur Isaac. Upon arriving, he opened the chapel, and rang the bell to let the local people know that Mass would commence shortly. The faithful began to flock into the church. But the first one in, although not a stranger to the people, was a stranger to the Church. It was John du Bois, who also wasn't quite sure why he was there.

As the priest began the Offertory, he unfolded the corporal and placed it in position for the Consecration. As he began to pray, the priest noticed a piece of the large Host on the corporal that he had consecrated the previous Tuesday during the Mass. This was the same day that the Lord appeared to John the first time. A rush of fear went through the priest's body. He realized that he must have dropped It onto the corporal during the Mass, and had just folded It into the corporal when he finished the celebration. He tried to remove the Host from the corporal. He planned to consume It after the Consecration. However, it seemed that the Host was stuck to the corporal. It wouldn't come loose. As he tried to pry It off, Fresh Blood began dripping from the Host. It didn't change in appearance. It was still white. But Blood welled up all around It.

The priest felt his legs buckle beneath him. He could feel all his strength ebbing out of him. The room began to spin. He held onto the altar to steady himself. John du Bois saw what had happened, and rushed up to the altar. "Father, don't be afraid. This miracle comes from God." The priest looked at John incredulously at first; but he saw a look in John's eyes, and an inner strength that came from him. Fr. Peter was able to compose himself, and continue the Mass. He folded the corporal containing the Bleeding Host, and used a new corporal for the Mass. He kept looking at the folded corporal during the Mass, however, and noted that the bloodstain kept getting larger.

After the Mass, he unfolded the original corporal, to find that the blood was still flowing from the Host. The Host, still white in appearance, floated in the pool of blood. All the members of the congregation at Mass witnessed the miracle.

The priest grieved, believing that this was all his fault. Had he consumed the Host entirely, and not left the Sacred Piece in the corporal when he had celebrated Mass three days before, none of this would have happened.

Blood continued to flow from the Host for five days, until the Tuesday after Pentecost. It was not gushing, but a slow, steady flow. When it finally stopped, it covered an area of approximately 3 inches by 6 inches of the corporal. Within a few weeks, it had dried completely.

By this time, the local Church authorities had taken an interest in the miraculous corporal, and took it from the Church of Bois Seigneur Isaac to investigate it. The Bishop of Cambrai, Pierre d'Ailly, put the corporal through grueling tests, including soaking it in wine, milk and lye. The miraculous gift of the Lord held up under all these tests. How many members of the investigating team, or those in the Bishop's office had their strength renewed, as a result of Our Lord allowing Himself to be soaked, prodded, and burned in lye?

In the meantime, what happened to John du Bois, our young playboy? He became zealous. For six years, he pleaded with the Bishop, used his influence as a nobleman, turned heaven and earth upside down for the miraculous corporal to be returned to the Chapel of the Woods. His family and friends considered him somewhat of an eccentric, obsessed by this bleeding altar cloth. The bishop knew he would have no peace until he gave in to the request of John du Bois. On May 3, 1411, the auxiliary bishop consecrated the chapel in honor of the Precious Blood, Our Lady, and also St. John the Baptist. The Eucharistic Miracle was returned to the chapel.

John du Bois was pleased, but it seemed he never forgave himself for not being sensitive to Our Lord those first two nights He appeared to him in the form of the Young Man. Looking back, he could not understand how he couldn't possibly have known that it was the Lord begging him for help. John du Bois continued bothering Bishop d'Ailly, who later became a Cardinal. After more than two years of pestering by John du Bois, on September 23, 1413, the Cardinal opened an investigation to officially confirm the authenticity of the miracle.

The Cardinal called himself a simple believer, completely convinced personally that Divine intervention had brought about the Eucharistic Miracle at Bois Seigneur Isaac. But he wanted to proceed according to canonical law. So the ordeal for the Lord, and for John du Bois began again. However, Jesus did not allow too long an ordeal, because 17 days later, on October 10, 1413, a Papal Bull was issued confirming the authenticity of the miracle. The Cardinal also ordered that a procession take place each year on the first Sunday following the Feast of the Birth of Our Lady, combining the Eucharistic Miracle with the honor Mary had been given at the Chapel, prior to the Miraculous event. The procession has been held every year from that time to this, except during the French Revolution, and perhaps during the Nazi Occupation of Belgium.

The Eucharistic Miracle is still on display in the Church in the little village of Ittre, Belgium. Pilgrims from all over Europe have come to this shrine to venerate the special gift the Lord gave us, all because a priest was careless almost 600 years ago. Or was that the reason?

Walldurn, 1330:
The Thorn-Crowned Head

The Lord must get very frustrated with us at times. He constantly gives us gifts which we either take for granted, or ignore completely. Often we're not even aware that we've been given a gift.

Do we judge these gifts from Jesus, His Body and Blood manifested in Eucharistic Miracles, as being meant for people from another time, another place, to fill another need? *No, these gifts are for us, for this time and this place.* The need is greater now than ever before. We have to accept and spread the Good News of Jesus, with us now and forever, to the whole world. When we reject or ignore Jesus' gifts, take them for granted, or worse, try to "hide them under a bushel basket", He is wounded yet again.

Such may have been the case in the little town of Walldurn, Germany, at the beginning of the fourteenth century. The thirteenth, fourteenth and fifteenth centuries in Europe were extremely difficult times for the Church. Small pockets of religious unrest plagued the Church of Germany. An undercurrent of unrest was felt as Germany entered into the fourteenth century. By the sixteenth century, Europe was engulfed in the

Protestant Reformation. Martin Luther was its author, but he was quickly imitated by so many others that today we have over 3000 splinters of the true Church.

The Lord gave us many Eucharistic Miracles in the fourteenth century, to combat "Anti-Eucharist" heresies throughout Europe. Every time He manifested Himself in this form, the miracle was always followed by a renewed reverence for the Eucharist, and a general return to the Church and the Sacraments.

The Lord gave us one of these special gifts in the year 1330, in the little town of Walldurn, between Frankfurt and Wurzburg. But it almost backfired on Him. An elderly priest, Heinrich Otto, was celebrating Mass at the Church of St. George in Walldurn. After he raised the host and chalice for the Consecration, he bumped into the Chalice, spilling the contents, the Precious Blood of Jesus, onto the corporal. He was concerned by his clumsiness, but his concern turned to shock when he saw what appeared on the corporal. The wine had turned into actual Blood, forming a design of the Crucified Christ, surrounded by eleven heads of Jesus crowned with Thorns.

Fr. Otto was unnerved. His entire body shook. Instinctively, he wanted to hide his blunder, the spilling of the Blood of Jesus on the corporal. He couldn't think of the accident as a blessing from above to be shared. The best thing he could have done would have been to hold up the Miraculous Corporal to the Congregation, praising the Lord for having given this gift to the people of the Church of St. George, through the unworthy means of Fr. Otto. He should have, but he didn't. He pushed the Corporal to the side, and continued with the Mass. We don't really know what emotions the priest was experiencing, other than shame and guilt for having caused the accident.

When the Mass was finished, and the congregation had left the church, Fr. Otto once again opened the Corporal, to see if his eyes had been playing tricks on him when the accident occurred. The scene portrayed by the Lord in this Miraculous painting was even clearer than it had been the first time. Jesus was on the Cross, in the Crucified Form. Surrounding Him were eleven heads of the Crucified Christ, all crowned with Thorns. The priest stared at the Heavenly Image for what seemed to be eternity. He looked around the Church. He was quite alone. He took the Corporal and hid it in a table under the Altar. He was very thorough in his concealment, to be sure that no one would ever find it.

Yet the priest might have recognized that this miracle was intended for others. First, this was a very unique message from Our Lord. The Image Jesus left on the corporal had to be very significant. Why eleven heads of Jesus Crowned with Thorns surrounding the Crucified Christ? In most of the Eucharistic Miracles we've researched, the meaning of the sign from Our Lord is clear, and easily understandable. This is the only Eucharistic Miracle where such a prophetic or symbolic message from God is given to us. What did it mean? Two explanations come to mind immediately. *Eleven* of the Apostles deserted Jesus at the Crucifixion. Only John the Beloved grieved at the foot of the Cross. *Eleven* of the twelve Apostles died the death of martyrs for Jesus. Only John the Beloved died of old age.

Second, the priest suffered great mental anguish from the time of the miraculous occurrence until he finally shared the secret. Shortly after the incident, he became sick. He could not get the Image of the corporal out of his mind. It haunted him day and night. He knew he should not have hidden the miracle. The longer he agonized over it, however, the worse he thought his situation would be if he finally confessed. He came to realize that the miracle was to be shared by the entire Church. But still he hesitated.

Death approached. The priest knew that he couldn't die without releasing himself from this sin of omission which had haunted him from the day it happened. He called in a fellow priest, and confessed the entire incident to him. He begged the priest to wait until he had died, and then remove the corporal from its hiding place. It had to be shared by all the people. In

At Walldurn, the spilled Blood formed pictures of Christ
Crucified surrounded by eleven Heads crowned with thorns (a
drawing of the Sacred Corporal).

that way, they could be strengthened in their faith in the Physical Presence of Christ in the Eucharist. Fr. Otto felt that by doing this, he would be exonerated from his sin. His fellow priest gave him absolution. Fr. Otto died peacefully immediately after having said his penance.

The priest to whom Fr. Otto had confessed, and some of his fellow priests, rushed into the Church to see for themselves this miracle of which Fr. Otto had spoken. They went to the hiding place, the table under the altar, and found the Blood-stained Corporal. It was as Fr. Otto had told them. The blood was still there, and the design of the Crucified Christ surrounded by 11 heads, crowned with Thorns. The priests knelt in reverence to this magnificent miracle with which the Lord had gifted them.

In a solemn ceremony, the corporal was put on display for the faithful to venerate. It became a place of pilgrimage for Germans and Europeans alike. Pilgrims by the thousands came to Walldurn to venerate the Sacred Corporal. Jesus, for His part, rewarded the pilgrims with many miracles, healings and conversions. There was a general return to the Sacraments, especially the Eucharist.

In 1445, the Eucharistic Miracle of Walldurn was sent to Rome to be investigated by the Vatican authorities. Pope Eugene IV, who had authenticated another Eucharistic Miracle, that of Ferrara, Italy, three years earlier, was very interested in inspecting this miracle. The priests of Walldurn brought all the documents that had been written about the corporal from the time the priests first removed it from the table under the Altar. The priest who had heard the confession of Fr. Otto had written all that Fr. Otto had told him about the miracle.

Pope Eugene IV confirmed and authenticated the Eucharistic Miracle of Walldurn, and bestowed a Plenary Indulgence on anyone who venerated the corporal during the octave of the Feast of Corpus Christi. The sacred cloth was returned to Walldurn in triumph. A beautiful church was built in honor of the Eucharistic Miracle. The corporal is venerated on the main altar of the church. Over the centuries, a number of hardened sinners has been known to enter the Church, and immediately repent their sins, searching out confessors in tears.

Devotion to this Eucharistic Miracle has continued over the years, through the Protestant Reformation and many wars, including two World Wars. In June 1985, the 650th Anniversary of the miraculous occurrence, festivities were held for the entire month. The corporal is not as bright and colorful today as it was 650 years ago. It has become dull, and yet the image of Our Lord Crucified is still visible. Perhaps It had to be bright and vibrant in that time to do the work the Lord had planned for It. Perhaps today is the right time for It to become bright again. Or maybe there's another Eucharistic Miracle happening in another part of the world where Our Lord feels the need for conversion. Maybe it's here in the United States.

Erding, 1417:
Reparation for Sacrilege

Originally, this was called the Miracle of Regensburg-Deggendorf-Erding, because it was on the road from Deggendorf to Regensburg that the miracle took place. This is an area of Bavaria just north of Munich. Today, this is a part of Germany, but at that time, it was the Kingdom of Bavaria.

Bavaria is the magnificent, storybook part of Germany that we read about in Grimms' Fairy Tales. It has always maintained the atmosphere of the Tyrolean Alps, the Beer Halls, the quaint chalets, the down comforters, the cobblestone streets. The Castles of Neuschwanstein and Hohenschwangau, built by King Ludwig and his father, were models for the castle in Disneyland. The people of Bavaria have always been known for their reverence for the Catholic Church. The southern part of Germany remained loyal to the Pope and the Catholic Church throughout the Protestant Reformation, and the various wars which later devastated Germany.

The main character in our narrative is a farmer, whose name is not known. He was a devout Catholic, receiving the Eucharist whenever he was able. Life was hard for him. No matter how he tried, he could not make ends meet. One day during

Lent in 1417, he walked to the Church of St. Peter in Alten Erding (Old Erding) with another farmer friend, whose fortunes had been much better than our farmer. He shared the difficult times he was having.

The farmer started to explain, "If the harvest is good, the grapes are bad. If the chestnuts do well, the olives are rotten. The cows give milk; but the sheep have little wool, and they don't bear lambs. I have never known good fortune; I have not even seen it from a distance. They say fortune has long hair like a horse. I have never been able to catch it."

He continued, "I'm experiencing extreme poverty. I'm ashamed to tell you about it. There are times when, in order to save my wife and children from hunger, I do without food for myself. I'm not afraid of hard work. I've known what it's like to work through the day and into the night. And yet, I can't seem to get ahead."

The farmer concluded, "Tell me, my friend, what is the secret of your success? You seem to do well. Your life seems to be in good order. Do you have a secret charm? If so, will you share your secret with me, so that I may have some success in my life?"

The other farmer looked at his walking companion with sympathy. He answered, "I keep the Blessed Sacrament in the little chapel of my house, day and night, all year long." What he was trying to tell the other farmer was that the Lord was the ruler of his life. He kept *Jesus in the chapel of his heart.* The house that safeguarded the chapel of his heart was his body. He was speaking in symbols, but the other man was too simple to understand the message.

The poor farmer thought he had been given the secret charm he had been searching for. As we said before, he was not a bad man. He just wasn't very intelligent. He saw how well the other man lived. The man attributed his success to the Blessed Sacrament. This farmer also believed in the power of Our Lord Jesus in the Eucharist. It made sense to him that if he had the

Lord with him at all times, in his house, his fortune would change.

The farmer worked the plan out in his mind over and over again. He fantasized how he would execute the scheme. He continued in his mind, imagining how his life would change after he secured his lucky charm, the Blessed Sacrament.

His opportunity came on Holy Thursday of that year. On the anniversary of the day that Our Lord Jesus gave us the Eucharist, the farmer thought to literally take this gift, and change his life. He brought a clean linen cloth to Church with him. He would put the Sacred Body of Christ into that cloth. It was washed and ironed just that day.

At Communion time, he nervously followed the crowd up to Communion. He feared that all eyes were on him. He looked around cautiously as he walked in line up to the Altar Rail. He knelt and waited for the priest to come to him. Beads of sweat broke out on his forehead. His eyes narrowed. His body shook. He was afraid he wouldn't be able to accomplish his plan. As the priest approached him, the farmer watched his eyes to see if the priest noticed anything unusual about him.

The Host was put on his tongue. He got up and left the altar, but didn't close his mouth. He went to a corner of the church, where he could take the Host out of his mouth, and place it in the clean kerchief without being noticed. It had not gotten wet from his tongue. All had gone according to plan. He left the church, proud of his triumph. He was joyful as he began the trip back to his home. He anticipated his new found fortune.

His conscience began working on him almost immediately. Was what he had done a sin? We reiterate here that he was a man of simple belief. He had very little or no instruction in our Faith. He was fervent, but completely uneducated. He believed instinctively. Each time he accused himself, he justified his actions. Had he committed a sin? Perhaps, but his intentions were good. He only wanted to make things better for his family. Before long all he could think about was the sin, and possible consequences. He had heard that sacrilege was not only an unforgivable sin, but that sacrilege theft was a criminal offense against the state. He also thought he remembered something about the death penalty for such a crime.

He was a nervous wreck by the time he decided to turn around, go back to the Church and confess his sin. He hoped that by turning himself in immediately he would show signs of repentance and good faith. He was sure the priest would deal with him mercifully. As he turned around to go back in the direction of Erding, the Host slipped out of the linen cloth, floated high into the air, and then plummeted to the earth. When it hit the ground, it disappeared. The farmer panicked. He looked all over the ground for the Host, but it was nowhere to be seen.

He ran back to the Church at breakneck speed. The priest was talking to members of the congregation as the farmer arrived, out of breath, and obviously out of sorts. He told his sin to the priest, going into great detail about how the Host flew up into the air, and then came back to earth. The priest wasted no time in running out onto the road, with the farmer and half the town in hot pursuit. From a distance, the priest could see the Host on the ground, gleaming, visible from far off. As the priest converged on the Host to pick It up, the Body of Our Lord Jesus flew up into the air again, stayed there for a time, and then plunged to the earth and disappeared, as It had done the first time.

The Bishop of the area was informed of the miracle. He came out to the place in the road where it had occurred, followed by a large group of his priests, plus a great crowd from the town of Erding. When the bishop approached the holy spot, the Host gleamed again, and took to the air for a third time. This time, possibly to impress the bishop, the Host remained suspended in the air for a long time. All eyes were glued to the Host. The bishop tried his best to catch hold of the Host, but to no avail. Finally, the Host fluttered, and returned to the earth to disappear for the last time. It was not seen again.

The large assemblage of faithful dropped to their knees in

prayer. The Holy Spirit spoke first through one of them, and then through the whole group. This was a sign from Our Lord that He wanted the Blessed Sacrament to be venerated in this place in a special way. They told the bishop and the pastor of the church that they were going to build a special chapel here. It was to be in honor of the Blessed Sacrament, and in penance for the sacrileges and blasphemies which had been committed against Our Lord in this most vulnerable form. They marked out the spot, and, as a community, built a beautiful church.

News of the miracle spread all over Bavaria, even into parts of Germany and Austria. The new church of Erding, in honor of the Blessed Sacrament, became a place of pilgrimage. The bishop gave his approval, and bestowed graces on pilgrims who venerated the Blessed Sacrament in this special church.

The Lord used what we would call "the least of my children" an ignorant farmer, to do His work in Erding. How often has He done that? We think of the little boy at Tabgha in Galilee, who had two fish and five barley loaves. The Lord was able to use that child to accomplish a great miracle, that of the multiplication of loaves and fishes. We think of St. Bernadette, St. Francis, St. Augustine, all self-proclaimed wretches, unworthy to be used for anything. How the Lord worked through them. The next natural question is "How unworthy, how useless are you and I? What great things can the Lord accomplish through us, if we let Him?"

Where you find the Son, you will always find the Mother. Erding is no exception to that rule. Less than 100 miles from this town is a German shrine, called Altotting. This is a Marian Shrine, consisting of an old Romanesque chapel, containing a sacred image, and two pilgrim churches from the thirteenth and fifteenth century. It's a very famous pilgrimage place in Upper Bavaria. Very often, pilgrimages combine visits to the two shrines.

Amsterdam, 1345: Safe in the Fire

When we visit Amsterdam today, we see a thriving port city, one of the most important shipping centers of Europe. It is the capital of the Netherlands. It is a large metropolis which has retained much of the beauty of the Holland we conjure up in our minds, a maze of canals, tulips, windmills, wooden shoes clanging across its many bridges. This would be a perfect setting for a Eucharistic Miracle.

However, the Amsterdam of 1345, when the Lord did manifest Himself in a Eucharistic Miracle consisted of four streets and a few alleys lined up along the main canal. It was a fishing village. There were small modest fishermen's huts, a church, and a monastery. The monastery was the largest building in the city. The Eucharistic Miracle given to this tiny village on March 13, 1345, was the beginning of the growth for which Amsterdam is now famous. As a matter of fact, on the 600th anniversary of the miracle, March 13, 1945, the Dutch Catholics attributed all the growth and progress of their city to the Eucharistic Miracle.

A fisherman on his deathbed called for a priest to come to his home to give him the last rites of the Church and Holy Communion. After having heard the man's confession, the priest blessed him with the oils of Extreme Unction, and gave him Communion.

The priest had no sooner left than the sick man began coughing violently. His wife ran over to him in an effort to help him. But the husband, gagging and choking beyond control, coughed up the Host, intact.

The wife reacted instinctively. She picked up the Host, and threw It into the fireplace. She didn't know why she had done it, and wished she hadn't. But the fire was raging, and she was not about to put her hands into it for fear of burning herself. That night she slept fitfully, tossing and turning. She was afraid she had committed some terrible sin. She had nightmares about the Sacred Host she had thrown into the fire.

The following morning, as soon as she got out of bed, she went over to the fireplace. The fire was not extinguished yet, but it was not as hot as the night before. She stoked the ashes, looking for the Eucharist. To her amazement she saw the Host sitting atop a burning ember. It was not burned at all. It had not even turned color. It was gleaming, brighter than the fire. She couldn't move. She knelt in adoration and thanksgiving before Our Lord in the Eucharist.

After a few minutes, she put her hands into the fire to retrieve the Body of her Lord, Whom she thought she had profaned. The fire had started to grow again, but she never felt any pain, nor did she burn her hands or arms. She wrapped the gleaming white Host in a cloth, and placed It in a linen chest.

She called the priest who had been to her house the previous night. She told him the story. She took the Host out of the linen chest, and handed It to him. The priest thought it best not to tell anyone about the incident, so as not to stir up scandal involving the woman or her husband. He took the Host, wrapped in the cloth, and returned It to the church, where he placed It in the tabernacle.

The following morning, the woman opened her linen chest to find that the same Host was still there. She went into a state of shock. She knew the priest had taken It away the day before. Had she committed such a terrible sin, that the Lord brought back the proof to punish her with the sight of It? She ran to the Church, *and explained what had happened to the priest. While she was in a panic, he smiled knowingly. The Lord had spoken to him. This miracle was not for him alone, or for his community. It was for the Church, the People of God. The priest was not allowed to hide it in a Tabernacle. Jesus wanted to use this miracle to awaken His sleeping people. The Miraculous Host was a light which was to shine all over Europe.*

The priest told his fellow friars about the miracle, as well as the people of the town. The townspeople spread the story to the surrounding villages. When the priest formed a procession to go to the fisherman's house for the Sacred Host, a huge crowd followed him and his fellow priests. They carried the Sacred Host back to the church of St. Nicholas affording Our Lord the honor He deserved for giving such a rich gift to these humble people.

There is a very funny element in this story. The fisherman who had been dying, to whom the priest brought the Eucharist on that first night, didn't die. To the contrary, he got better and better each day. However, when word of the miracle reached the ears of the townspeople, and those from other villages, they all went to the fisherman's house to see where the miracle had taken place. It became sort of a shrine.

We don't know for sure what the temperament of the fisherman had been prior to the miracle. We know that he had put his house in order, and was anticipating his trip to Heaven. He had been forgiven all his sins. He had received the Last Sacraments of the Church. Now, he found himself not only not dead, but the victim of pilgrims and curiosity seekers. His wife, on the other hand, was flattered with all the attention she was getting. His temper flared. He and his wife had a heated argument. Their child, not wanting to get into the middle of it, sat over by the fireplace to get out of the line of fire. The argument became so animated that the husband and wife were running all over the house. The little boy was knocked into the fireplace, and burned himself. The father rescued him from the fire, and the incident ended the argument between the child's parents.

Out of sheer terror, the child began to convulse. From that time on, whenever he became nervous, he lapsed into convulsions. This lasted until his father, the fisherman, finally went to the Church of St. Nicholas to venerate the Eucharistic Miracle, of which he had been an integral part. When he venerated the Sacred Host, his anger left him, and his son's convulsions left him.

An investigation by the Church began immediately. Within a few months, the Bishop of Utrecht officially declared that an authentic miracle had occurred in the little town of Amsterdam. In the same pastoral letter, he authorized veneration of the Eucharistic Miracle of the Host. The little house of the fisherman was converted into a Chapel, in which the Miraculous Host was placed. It was called the Chapel of the Sacrament. The fireplace of the fisherman's hut was kept intact, and became a permanent part of the new shrine.

A second miracle took place 100 years later. Amsterdam had grown considerably in the century since the first miracle had taken place. On May 24, 1452 the entire city of Amsterdam was engulfed in fire. Most of the buildings were destroyed by the blaze. When the Chapel of the Blessed Sacrament (the former fisherman's hut) caught fire, some of the parishioners made an attempt to save the Miraculous Host from destruction by the flames. They tried to force open the tabernacle. The Host had been placed in a beautiful monstrance, which was inside the tabernacle. The heat of the Church was becoming unbearable. The workers worked feverishly, but to no avail. The heat of the fire had made it impossible to get the door open. As the roof of the Chapel began to cave in, the men ran out of the Church to safety, their mission a failure.

The entire Church burned to the ground, including the tabernacle. There was a great sadness among the faithful of the city, especially those who had tried in vain to rescue the Eucharistic Miracle. The next day, they sifted through the ashes of the Church, hoping against hope, that something remained of their precious

Host. Their grief turned to joy as they spotted the Monstrance, completely unscathed, there among the ashes of the Church. Even the silk veil which covered the Monstrance had been saved from the fire. So, once again the Lord saved the same Host from fire in the same house in Amsterdam.

A new chapel was built, more elaborate and more beautiful than the previous one. The fame of the Eucharistic Miracle of Amsterdam, now called the twofold miracle, spread beyond the Netherlands to all of Europe. The Hapsburg Emperor of the Holy Roman Empire, Maxmillian, went to Amsterdam in pilgrimage to the Eucharistic Miracle. He prayed for a healing at the shrine, which was granted him. He showed his thanksgiving by donating beautiful gifts to the Chapel of the miracle.

Amsterdam and the Eucharistic Miracle became a major place of pilgrimages and processions from the time of the second miracle in 1452. They took place all year long, but in particular during the Octave of the Feast, March 13. This continued as a strong practice in Amsterdam up until 1578, when Calvinism took hold in Holland, and all religious pilgrimages and processions were outlawed. The persecutions were able to stop the physical manifestations of praise to Our Lord Jesus in the Eucharistic Miracle, but they could not stop the burning in the hearts of the Catholics. The story of the miracle, and the tradition of the processions were handed down from generation to generation.

When the persecutions ended, the feast in honor of the Eucharistic Miracle was resumed, but not in public. There was still a fear of recrimination which stayed with the people. However, on the occasion of the three hundredth anniversary of the miracle, 1645, the feast was celebrated with the same enthusiasm and ceremony in which it had been celebrated before the Protestants had taken hold in Holland.

The practice of walking in procession on the anniversary of the miracle has remained with the people of Amsterdam to the present day. Even during the occupation of Holland by the

Nazis, just prior to the 600th anniversary of the miracle, pilgrims walked at night in secret procession, risking death at the hands of the Nazis, praising Our Lord Jesus for the gift of the Sacred Host.

Was this miracle just for the people of Amsterdam? Throughout the history of this unusual Eucharistic Miracle, one thing has been made very clear by the Lord. It was to be spread all over Europe. People from the entire continent were to come to Amsterdam in pilgrimage to this special gift from the Lord. The purpose was not to venerate ancient history. Jesus showed us through the miracle itself, and the ongoing dedication to Him in this miracle, even in the face of death, during the Protestant Religious Persecutions and the Nazi occupation, that He is with us now, as He was on March 13, 1345, and as He was 2,000 years ago.

Langenwiese, 1400's:
All Creation Honors Him

The Lord gives us a new cast of characters leading up to the Eucharistic Miracle which took place in Langenwiese, in an area called Silesia, between Poland and Czechoslovakia. Again, He uses people from other countries to do His work in an area completely foreign to the people involved.

Enter a young man called Giantedesco, John the German, or better known, especially by Californians, as San Juan Capistrano, John of Capistran. He was called John the German because his father was of Germanic background and, although John was Italian, he looked like a German count. A brilliant man, he got a degree in law in Perugia, near Assisi, and became Governor of Perugia at the age of 26. His priorities were anything but religious, until he was taken prisoner during a local war between the Perugians and the Malatestas. His story inside prison is much like that of St. Francis, although it took place some 200 years later. He began to consider the values of his life, and upon being released from prison, decided to change his life, and join the Franciscans.

The life of St. John is exciting enough on its own to make a good story, but in order to keep our focus, we have to limit ourselves to his involvement with this Eucharistic Miracle. Suffice it to say, however, that he was so blocked in entering into the religious life that men of lesser courage would not have endured. He was greatly helped during this time by St. Bernadine of Siena.

St. Bernardine of Siena, a driving force in the Franciscan Order, had a fervent devotion to the Eucharist. His symbol, a Host with rays of Blazing Sun and the letters IHS, is seen on many churches in Italy, mostly in Siena. As a matter of fact, in the famous Piazza Del Campo in Siena, the symbol is emblazoned on the top of the main building. It is also seen in Florence on the Palazzo Vecchio. A great part of St. Bernardine's ministry was devoted to defense and instruction of the Eucharist.

St. John became one of St. Bernardine's students. Through St. Bernardine's influence, he developed his passion for the Eucharist, and our Lord Jesus. After he left St. Bernardine, he went out on his own to fight for the conversion of heretics, and to correct the grave errors they were spreading. He developed a reputation for holiness on his own. Crowds of faithful gathered to hear him wherever he spoke. He's been given credit for turning hundreds of thousands back to the faith by his sermons. He is also known to have had great healing powers.

Over the years, he was given uncommon authority by the Vatican to do battle with heretics, schismatics, and those involved with witchcraft and the occult. He was very stern in his dealings with enemies of the Church, and was considered an apostle, a prophet. No matter where he went, the faithful flocked to touch him, hear him, ask him to heal their sick. He gave credit for all healings to the intervention of the relics of St. Bernardine, which he carried with him.

Towards the end of his life, the Pope sent St. John to the area of Bavaria, Austria, and Poland to defend the faith. A group of heretics led by John Huss and called Hussites were then active, forerunners of Luther. Among the errors they spread was a disbelief in the physical presence of Jesus in the

Eucharist. This heresy had become very strong in the area of Austria and Poland. St. John spent all his time fighting these heretics. As if that was not enough, he also recruited an army to stop the onslaught of the Turks, which was imminent.

We have now set the stage for the miracle, and very possibly for understanding the reason for the miracle. While St. John was in Breslau, he celebrated Mass and spoke out strongly against the Anti-Eucharist movement, which was spreading in Breslau. After he left the church, thieves, influenced by the heretics, broke into the church and stole some Hosts St. John had consecrated, from the Tabernacle. It is believed that their purpose was to desecrate and blaspheme the Sacred Hosts. They wrapped Them in a white linen cloth. The Hosts started to bleed profusely, the blood pouring out of the cloth. The thieves, fearing for their lives if they were caught, and realizing that they were not able to destroy the Hosts, went out onto one of the roads leading into Langenwiese. They hid the Hosts in the forest. They picked what they considered to be the most desolate spot around. There was no way, they thought, for anyone to find the Bleeding Hosts. They did not take into consideration Our Lord, Whom they had blasphemed. He used this sacrilege to provide us with an additional miracle in the way the Hosts were found.

Shortly after the thieves hid the Hosts, a Polish man was traveling towards Langenwiese in a carriage drawn by four horses. At a certain spot in the road, the horses stopped abruptly, and knelt down. The driver could not understand what caused the animals to act in this manner. He got out to investigate. The horses remained in their kneeling position. As the man searched the area, he found the blood soaked bundle with the Hosts inside.

The Polish man contacted the local priest, who went out to the place where the Hosts were buried. The priest, followed by a group of local people, took the bundle with the Hosts and brought Them back in solemn procession to the Church of Langenwiese. The news of the miracle spread throughout the district.

We've learned that nothing is accidental with the Lord.

The plan which the Lord had set into motion included a parallel event taking place at this time hundreds of miles away.

Constantinople had fallen to the Turks at the time of this miracle, between Easter and Pentecost in the year 1453. They were marching north to capture all of Europe, and enslave Christianity under the sword of the Muslims. Pilgrims were drawn to the Church of the Eucharistic Miracle in Langenwiese. Prayers and petitions were offered to the Lord to halt the invasion of the Turks. The official feast was designated as the Fourth Sunday after Easter. At one time, as many as 50,000 pilgrims were reported to have come on pilgrimage to Langenwiese, to pray for the forgiveness of the sins of man, and for deliverance from the Turks.

The turning point against the Turks was at Belgrade in 1456. The Europeans had prepared for their attack. St. John Capistrano, near death by this time, had finally gathered together his army of men. Armed with prayer on the battlefield, and an enormous amount of prayer and penance at the Shrine, the Turks were defeated, and Europe was saved.

We truly believe that the Lord has a teaching for us in everything that goes on in the world. If all we learn from these Eucharistic Miracles is a lesson of the past, what have we really learned? Our Lady has been pleading with us for centuries in her apparitions to listen to her Son. She vocalizes what the Lord has been trying to teach us in these supernatural manifestations. Yet we keep looking for signs.

If the Lord were to manifest Himself again today in a Eucharistic Miracle, would we pay attention to it, or keep looking for another sign? In Luke 16:31, Jesus says "They will not be convinced even if one should rise from the dead." But then again, in the very next chapter, Luke 17:5, He tells us, "If you had faith the size of a mustard seed, you could say to this sycamore 'Be uprooted and transplanted into the sea', and it would obey you."

Eucharistic Miracles and the Saints

Who are the Saints? They are our brothers and sisters in Christ, role models who lived many years ago. The saints are you and me of another time. One common thread that binds the saints together, that makes them the communion of saints, is the very special relationship they shared with Jesus. For our purposes in this chapter, we want to concentrate on saints who had a very obvious passion for the Eucharist. Their entire lives revolved around their strong Faith in the Physical Presence of Jesus in the Eucharist. We want to share some Eucharistic Miracles of a different sort, involving these special friends of Jesus, His saints. First, we will describe three unique miracles, and then we will turn to the many holy persons who have lived for long periods on the Eucharist alone.

St. Anthony of Padua

While St. Francis of Assisi is the official Patron Saint of Italy, St. Anthony of Padua is the most honored saint in all of Italy, and he was not even Italian. He was born in Lisbon, Portugal, which is the reason for the Feast of St. Anthony of Lisbon being celebrated on June 13, the same day as the Feast of St.

Anthony of Padua. St. Anthony lived in the early 13th century.

Beginning as a humble dishwasher, Anthony became one of the greatest homilists in Europe, as well as Defender of the Eucharist. But in Rimini, on the Adriatic Sea, to the southeast of Padua, he was not faring well. The heretics made fun of him; when he spoke of the Eucharist, they laughed hysterically, ridiculing him.

St. Anthony was known for his sharp temper. When the heretics poked fun at him as he spoke at the port of Rimini, he turned toward the sea, and delivered his homily to the fish. The fish, for their part, raised their bodies out of the water, and perched, as it were, on top of the water, listening to the homily given by St. Anthony. When he was finished, St. Anthony blessed the fish; at which point they returned to the sea.

The enemies of the Church, on seeing this, were completely overwhelmed. Word spread throughout the town, and heretics by the droves were converted. But there was one man, Bonvillo by name, who wasn't impressed with St. Anthony's persuasive ways. He said to him, "You, who hold fish spellbound, let's see if you can do the same to my mule." A challenge was made. The heretic would starve his mule for three days. At the end of that time, St. Anthony would stand on one end of the square, holding the Eucharist, and Bonvillo on the other, with a pail of the animal's favorite fodder. If the mule went to St. Anthony first, the heretic would stop persecuting Catholics.

The beast was starved for three days. St. Anthony fasted and prayed for three days. On the third day, St. Anthony celebrated Mass at the local church. After the Mass, he took a Consecrated Host with him out into the square. It was packed with heretics on one side, and converts on the other. Bonvillo had his mule by his side, tempting him with the pail of fodder. At the given time, St. Anthony crossed to one corner of the square with the Eucharist in his hand. The heretic went off to the other side, with the pail of delicious smelling food in his hands. He tried luring the mule with the food.

St. Anthony spoke softly to the animal. He gave him a little sermon. He said "Creature of God, in His name, I command you to come here to adore Him, so that it will give truth to all of the Real Presence of Jesus in the Blessed Sacrament of the Eucharist."

The mule ignored his owner and the food, and went instead over to where St. Anthony held the Body of Christ. He knelt down on both legs, and lowered his head in reverence. When all were convinced that the Lord had won out over the heretic, St. Anthony blessed the mule, who then got up, and proceeded to eat all the fodder in the pail.

The heretic Bonvillo followed the example of his mule. He went down on his knees, head bowed to the ground, in adoration of the Blessed Sacrament. There is a shrine in Rimini to this day in honor of the Eucharistic Miracle of St. Anthony and the Donkey.

St. Clare of Assisi

St. Clare was the first female Franciscan and founder of the Poor Clares, under the rule of St. Francis, in the 13th century. But Clare was so much more. She was the personification of Holy Poverty. She was Sister Moon to Francis' Brother Sun.

One day, Clare found her convent to be in great danger. The Convent of San Damiano stood between the troops of Frederick II and the city of Assisi, which they were preparing to attack. The fact that there was a group of virgin nuns in the convent was particularly appealing to the Saracen mercenaries in Frederick's army, who hated Christians and had an unnatural lust for Caucasian women. They proceeded to attack the Convent. Clare at this time, was in her bed, ill. Her ladies rushed to her, crying, in a state of panic. What would they do? Could she protect them from the attacking soldiers? One of the sisters ran into the room to report that she had seen soldiers in the fields right around the convent. A general state of alarm began.

Clare had two sisters help her up out of bed. She walked

St. Clare of Assisi (top) and a depiction of the Eucharistic Miracle of St. Anthony of Padua and the mule.

over to their little chapel, and removed a monstrance containing the Blessed Sacrament. She held it in her hands, pressed her head against it, and prayed to the Lord. She walked to the large open window facing the courtyard down below. She spoke to the Lord, and He answered her. She said: "Protect, Lord, these your servants, that I now, by myself, cannot protect." A very sweet voice, that of a young child, answered her, "I will take care of you always." St. Clare added another prayer. "My Lord, protect also, as it pleases you, this city that by your love supports us." The answer she received from the Lord was "It will have to go through sufferings, but it will be defended by my protection."

Strengthened by these words, Clare turned to her sister nuns, who were terrified by the prospects of the attack of the feared Saracens. "I guarantee you, my daughters, that you will not suffer any evil. Only have faith in Christ." She took the monstrance and held it high in the air.

The sound of guns ceased. The advancing Saracens stopped in their tracks at the courtyard of the Convent. They looked up at Clare, at the monstrance in her hand. As if they had seen the devil, they turned and fled, leaving the convent of San Damiano in peace. The next day, the people of Assisi were pleased but astonished that the Saracens had not attacked their city. They had left the area without ever setting foot in the town.

Clare admonished her ladies who had heard the voice of Jesus speaking to their Mother Superior; they were not to speak a word to anyone of what they had heard as long as she was alive.

The life of St. Clare is full of similar reports on the special bond that unfolded between her and Jesus. She felt the closest to Him in the Mass, and in the Eucharist. She could do without food, or drink. Material things had no value to her. But she could not be without Her Lord in the Mass and the Eucharist.

So it came to pass that on Christmas Eve, 1252, the year before she died, she was too ill to go to the Midnight Mass with her sisters. She could not get out of the bed. She lay there, very sad to be deprived of Our Lord Jesus in the Eucharist on this special night. Her thoughts brought her back to the time in Gubbio when Francis made the first Nativity Scene, after which all Nativity scenes in the future would be fashioned. Christmas had always been a very joyous time for both Clare and Francis. She missed not having him with her on earth, but especially at this important time.

Suddenly, she could smell the sweet fragrance of burning candles, and altar incense. She was taking part in the Midnight Mass at the Basilica. Then she was whisked off to the east, to the Bethlehem of 1,200 years before. She was brought down to the cave where the Infant Jesus was born. St. Joseph and Mary were there, in the company of the animals whose cave the Holy Family shared. Our Lord Jesus came to her as a grown man, and put the Sacred Host into her mouth. Finally, she was transported back to the Convent of San Damiano in Assisi.

St. Juliana Falconieri

The name Falconieri is famous in church annals. The uncle of St. Juliana, St. Alexis Falconieri, is one of the seven founders of the Servite Order. He was instrumental in the upbringing of St. Juliana, her father having died when she was very young.

Juliana founded the order of Servite nuns, and became the first superior. She was known for her great charity which aided in the reconciliation of enemies, the conversion of sinners, and the healing of the sick. She never asked her ladies to mortify themselves more than she herself did. As a matter of fact, no one was able to keep up with her zeal or mortification. She hindered her health greatly. Because of this, upon her death at age 70 her stomach was so weakened that she was not able to receive Our Lord Jesus in the Eucharist.

When the Saint lay on her death bed, she grieved that she was not able to receive the Lord in the Eucharist. She was beloved by the community, and by the priest in attendance at the end of her life. She still had a very strong will. She convinced the priest, Fr. James de Campo Reggio, to bring the Eucharist to her bedside, so that she could at least see Her Lord before she died. The priest agreed.

When he brought the Blessed Sacrament into the room, Juliana was obsessed with the desire to touch Him somehow. She pleaded with the priest to allow her to at least kiss the Host. He refused. She waited a little longer. It was very obvious to all that she was nearing death. She begged the priest to put a corporal on her chest, and just lay the Lord gently on her chest, near her heart. The priest, who found it very difficult to deny her anything, gave in. Fr. James arranged the cloth on her chest, as she had requested. No sooner had the Host been placed there than It disappeared from sight, to the astonishment of the 18 people gathered in the room. Saint Juliana closed her eyes, smiling. She never opened them again. At the touch of Our Lord Jesus on her heart, her life had been fulfilled, and she went to Him.

There was a hush in the room. They had all seen it, but no one could believe their eyes. All of the sisters in the room and the priest fell to their knees in reverence to the Miraculous Gift they had been given. They prayed for the safe journey of the soul of their foundress to her heavenly reward. In due time, her body was prepared for the funeral. Blessed Joan Solderini, who assumed the saint's responsibility in the community, was the first to notice another miracle. They took St. Juliana's bedclothes off the body. On her left breast was the outline of the Crucified Christ, encircled by the Host. It was in the same position as the Host which had been placed on her chest, and had disappeared.

St. Catherine of Siena

St. Catherine was a very special friend of Jesus. There was an intense closeness between the Saint and Our Lord. She was not formally educated, and yet because of her writings, she is one of only two women doctors of the Church. She professed to have been educated directly by Jesus. She was given the gift of holding the Baby Jesus in her arms, presented to her by Our Lady. She was mystically married to Jesus. She was given the gift of ecstasies and levitation many times during her life. She is responsible for the return of the popes from Avignon to Rome. There are volumes written about the saint. For our purposes here, however, we will confine ourselves to St. Catherine and the Eucharist.

St. Catherine had been the recipient of many apparitions from Jesus throughout her life. According to the Life of St. Catherine, written by Blessed Raymond of Capua, her confessor and confidant, in an apparition which took place about the year 1372 she was given a special gift, one which would stay with her for the rest of her life. She was allowed to drink of the Blood of Jesus, from His side. She shared with Blessed Raymond that after drinking the Blood of Jesus, she couldn't eat anymore. She was neither hungry, nor could she hold anything in her stomach, other than the Sacred Species, the Body and Blood of Jesus.

The saint died in 1380. For the seven year period prior to her death, she took no food into her body other than the Eucharist. Her fasting did not affect her energy, however. She maintained a very active life during those seven years. As a matter of fact, most of her greatest accomplishments occurred during that period. Her death had nothing to do with malnutrition, or anything connected with lack of food. She had a vision in the early part of 1380, in which the ship of the Church crushed her to the earth. She offered herself as a willing sacrifice. She was ill from this time until April 21 of that year, when she suffered a paralytic stroke from the waist down. On April 29, she went to her reward.

St. Catherine of Genoa

We speak of another Catherine, from another time and another place in Italy. This Catherine is completely different from Catherine of Siena, with one great exception, their common love for the Body and Blood of Our Lord Jesus in the Eucharist.

Catherine of Genoa had wanted to enter the religious life as a young girl, but this was not allowed by her father. She was subjected to a marriage of convenience, which didn't work out. For the first five years her husband was seldom home. His was a life of parties and affairs. For the next five years, in an effort to have some sort of life, Catherine tried to take part in the gaieties of her husband's world, but was unable to find any pleasure in it. She experienced a conversion on the evening before the feast of St. Benedict in 1473. The Lord had taken hold of her, and never let her go.

She became a daily communicant, which was unusual for that time. Only priests could receive communion daily without being accused of repenting for some scandal. However, once Catherine began this practice, she never stopped. Her love for Jesus became so great, and her desire for the Eucharist so strong, that she began the habit of refraining from any food all through Advent and Lent of each year. During these times, she lived on some water with salt, and the Sacred Species. This fasting had no effect on her physical capabilities. In 1507, however, at 60 years of age, she became very ill, and had to curtail all her fasting, as well as fast days set down by the Church. She lived to be 63 years old, and was very active for most of that time.

Blessed Elizabeth the Good

Blessed Elizabeth was one of the last of the medieval mystics. She was born in 1386 at Waldsee, in Wurtenberg. She had shown signs of deep spirituality at a very early age. Her parents gave her the nickname "Good Bessie" because of her outstanding behavior. At fourteen years of age, her confessor, Fr. Conrad Kugelin, suggested that she join the Third Order of St. Francis. She followed his advice, going to live with a woman weaver to learn the trade. Four years later, she and four other tertiaries formed a community at the recommendation of the priest. She stayed there for the rest of her life.

She was known to live a very austere life. She was also known for her fasting. It has been reported that on one occasion she went for as long as three years without food, and then only broke the fast because the devil came to her in the form of her confessor, and ordered her to stop. She fasted for a total of twelve years, or one third of her life. During these times, she lived on the Blessed Sacrament alone.

Blessed Angela of Foligno

Angela was part of the wave of piety and reform that took place in the wake of St. Francis of Assisi's work in Italy, and especially in the Umbrian Valley. Foligno is only about ten miles from Assisi. Angela was born less than twenty years after the death of St. Francis, the famous "Poverello". The Franciscan revival was very strong during her lifetime.

From the accounts of her early years, it would seem that Francis had no effect on her at all. Her behavior was the complete opposite of one who would embrace the Franciscan philosophy with a passion. She was married to a rich man. Her life was very worldly and careless. She not only accused herself of being pleasure seeking and self indulgent, but a great sinner. But when she did experience her conversion, it was complete.

She did not retreat from the world immediately, however. She talks about eighteen steps she had to take to bring her close to Jesus. As part of these steps, she had to shed all the worldly things that had been so important to her all her life. This was not an easy task. Each possession that she gave up felt like a tooth being pulled out of her mouth.

As she purified herself, she turned inward, depending less on outward influences and needs. It was at this time that she began fasting. In Butler's Lives of the Saints, it mentions that "She forgot to eat". There are reports that Blessed Angela lived for twelve years without taking any food, except the Holy Eucharist. She took only water in addition to the Blessed Sacrament.

Saint Nicholas of Flue

St. Nicholas of Flue is one of the most famous saints in Switzerland. He is also considered a great patriot. He was very religious all his life, having been born of pious parents. He was a soldier and statesman, father of ten children. He refused the honor of being appointed Governor on more than one occasion. One of his sons did become the Governor of the area. There was a religious brotherhood at the time in Germany, Switzerland and the Netherlands, called Friends of God (*Gottesfreunde*). They pledged strict loyalty to the Catholic Church. His family were members, as was his wife.

At 50 years of age, Nicholas expressed a desire to leave his home and family, and become a religious hermit. While this may not have been considered normal, the Friends of God recognized such vocations. So his wife and family did not oppose him. He put his house in order; and in the Fall of 1467, with nothing but a walking stick, a Rosary, and a grey-brown pilgrim's tunic, he set out on his new life. He was barefoot and bareheaded.

At the very beginning of his ministry as a hermit, lying under a tree one night, he suffered a severe attack of stomach spasms. The pain was so bad that Nicholas thought he would die. Praying intently, he accepted whatever the Lord's will would be. After a time, the pains passed, but from that time until the end of his life, some twenty years later, he lost all his desire for food or drink. He was not able to hold anything in his stomach except the Body and Blood of Our Lord Jesus in the Eucharist.

Though Nicholas was a hermit, he was very visible in the community. He set aside time every day to help people who came to his lonely dwelling with spiritual or worldly problems. His advice was also solicited in matters of state. In one particular situation where the Swiss government was on the verge of taking up arms to settle a territorial dispute, Nicholas' aid was sought. They accepted his wisdom, and war was averted. It became common knowledge that he did not eat or drink anything. When people asked him how he could live without any food, his only reply was "God knows". Many accounts were written about interviews with the saint during this period of fasting. One in particular, written by Albert Von Bonstetten, dean of the monastery at the shrine in Einsiedeln, described the saint as being tall, brown and wrinkled. His eyes were clear, his teeth white and preserved, and his appearance strong and healthy.

A great deal is written about St. Nicholas. He died in 1487, on his 70th birthday. He was proclaimed a saint immediately by the people of Switzerland, but the Vatican waited until 1669 to open the cause for his beatification, and it wasn't until 1947 that he was actually canonized. Perhaps because he was so involved with civic matters, his life was chronicled so completely. Whatever the reason, the fact that he lived for twenty years without food or drink is part of his biography, which was written by lay people of his country.

Blessed Lydwina of Schiedam

The more we research these special people who have received this gift of total abstinence except for the Blessed Sacrament, the more we become aware how exceptional their lives were. For the most part, they suffered great physical pain during their lifetime. In the case of Blessed Lydwina, it would seem that she took all the sins of man on her body. She is sort of a Dorian Gray in reverse. (*The Portrait of Dorian Gray* is the story of an extremely handsome man whose features never grew old. A painting of him took on all of his age and sins. At the time of his death, the portrait of Dorian Gray was hideous, from years of sinning.)

Blessed Lydwina was called and considered a saint during her lifetime. She has always been called Saint in her hometown, and throughout Holland. She has never been officially canonized a saint. She was beatified by the Church in 1890. She died in 1433.

Lydwina was a pretty girl of poor circumstances. Her parents were spiritual, as was Lydwina. She was a very normal, very pretty teenager. Nothing unusual was known about her until she reached sixteen years. By a strange quirk, she was accidentally knocked down on an ice skating pond and broke a rib. It was considered a very minor accident, but Lydwina never recovered from it. To the contrary, she fell victim to an internal abscess which burst, causing poisons to permeate her system. She vomited violently. This was followed by headaches, toothaches, and pains in every part of the body. She also experienced high fevers, and unquenchable thirst.

Her condition baffled the medical profession all during her lifetime. At the beginning of her long suffering, the doctors told her family that nothing they did helped her condition. Rather, all medical help seemed to worsen the girl's health.

It took three years of agony before Lydwina was informed by the Lord that He wanted her to suffer for the sins of man. This was to be her vocation from that time on. She lived in excruciating pain for the next 34 years. Her malady only got worse in that time, to the point where she couldn't move any part of her body other than her left arm. She was covered with abscesses. She was blind in one eye, and the other eye could not stand the glare of light brighter than the reflection of a fire Any time that medical means were used to alleviate pain in one part of her body, greater afflictions appeared in other parts of the body.

From the beginning of her illness, she had trouble taking food. She went from being able to eat a little solid food, to liquids, wine at first, and finally, only water. There is sworn testimony to the fact that she lived on nothing but the Eucharist for nineteen years. Keep in mind that she could not hold down any food. But in the same condition, sometimes on the same day, she would be given Our Lord Jesus in the Eucharist, and she could hold that down.

At the outset of her invalidism, she was only allowed to receive Communion twice a year. When the priest who counselled her, Fr. John Pot, became aware that Communion was really the only sustenance she had, he allowed her to receive every two months. Later on, it became once every two weeks. Consider, though, that this was all she lived on. It was reported that her strength seemed to come back somewhat after having received Communion. This is not to say that she got up and walked around, but her face took on some color. Her disposition appeared more pleasant. She was at peace with the world.

She was given special heavenly gifts which offset the life she lived. She was able to heal people, but not herself. She had the gift of prophecy, and was able to see things that were happening in other places. She had ecstasies, where she would be whisked off to Rome and Jerusalem. She helped Jesus carry His Cross on the Via Dolorosa. She was able to experience the pains of purgatory, and the joy of Heaven. Each time she had these out of body experiences, however, her sufferings became more intense. It was as if the Lord never wanted her to forget her true vocation, which was to suffer for the sins of man.

Many biographies have been written about Blessed Lydwina, including one by Thomas à Kempis, author of the famous *Imitation of Christ*.

Alexandrina da Costa

Someone who could be considered a modern day Blessed Lydwina is Alexandrina da Costa of Portugal. She was born in 1904 and died in 1955. She was crippled at fourteen, when she jumped out of a window to avoid being raped. Her spine snapped, causing irreparable damage. In 1924 she became totally paralyzed, confined to her bed for the rest of her life.

Her life has been compared to Blessed Lydwina because of her intense suffering; to St. Margaret Mary Alocoque, because of her conversations with Jesus; and to Therese Neumann, because she suffered the Passion of Jesus on Fridays.

She has not been venerated yet, which is not unusual. The Church takes many years before the cause for beatification of holy people are opened. In the case of Lydwina, who was called a saint during her lifetime, she died in 1433, but her cause was not opened until 1890. She has still not been canonized by the Church. St. Nicholas of Flue was considered a saint from the time of his death in 1487; yet the cause for his beatification was not opened until 1669, and his canonization took place in 1947. Padre Pio of Pietrelcina has been called the Saint of the 20th Century. He had all the gifts of Jesus, including the Stigmata, the Fragrance of Heaven, Bilocation, and was known to be the Perfect Confessor. He died in 1968, and the Cause for his beatification has only recently been opened.

Alexandrina lived on the Eucharist alone for thirteen years. She was the recipient of heavenly inner locution, in which she could feel the Lord speak to her. She had been given the gift of sharing the Passion of Jesus every Friday 180 consecutive times. However, in 1942, during Holy Week, the Passion Ecstasy stopped. Her pains became unbearable. She was nauseous constantly. She developed a voracious hunger and thirst, yet she couldn't hold any food in her stomach. Milk and some mineral water were the extent of what she could drink. She thought it was finally the end of her life.

This was the beginning of her thirteen year fast. However, unlike the other fasters we have written about, Alexandrina never lost the hunger and thirst she had felt on Holy Thursday of that week in 1942. It stayed with her all the time. She could not take food, but she was hungry.

This was not the Middle Ages, but the middle of the 20th Century. It is a fact that no one can live without food or water for more than 20 days. Yet here was a claim from this bedridden girl that after one year of total fasting, she was still alive. At the request of her doctor, and the local bishop, she submitted to medical observation in the hospital at Oporto, the nearest large city to Balasar, her town. It was supposed to end after 30 days. However, as the ordeal was almost at an end, one of the doctors insisted that his nurse watch her for another 10 days. She submitted to this additional torture. Her only requirement was that she be allowed to receive Holy Communion each day.

At the end of the forty days of scrutiny, both Dr. Araujo, who had originated the testing for 30 days, and Dr. Azevedo, who had insisted on the additional 10 day test, wrote certificates attesting to the fact that Alexandrina had been under 24-hour-a-day surveillance the entire time by impartial witnesses, and that she had not taken any food or drink in any period of time, except the Eucharist. The findings also stated that during this period of observation, she had maintained her weight; her breathing, temperature, blood pressure, pulse and blood were normal. It was determined that there was no scientific or medical explanation for this extraordinary and exceptional case.

Our Lord Jesus appeared to Alexandrina and explained to her what science could not. "You are living by the Eucharist alone because I want to prove to the world the power of the Eucharist, and the power of my life in souls."

On April 9, 1955, Alexandrina celebrated the 13th anniversary of her Eucharistic Fast. On the feast of the Miracle of the Sun, October 13, 1955, Alexandrina joined Our Lady of Fatima and Our Lord in heaven.

Theresa Neumann

Therese Neumann lives up to her famous namesakes, St. Therese of Lisieux, our Little Flower, and Santa Teresa la Grande d' Avila, one of only two women doctors of the Church. Therese Neumann was a remarkable woman. She may well be proclaimed a Saint of our Church, although not very likely in our lifetime.

Therese came from an area of Bavaria already blessed twice by the Lord, with the Eucharistic Miracle of Erding and the Marian shrine, Altotting. She was born just prior to midnight on Good Friday, April 8, 1898. She was baptized two days later on Easter Sunday, April 10. There were ten living children in the Neumann family, an eleventh having died soon after birth. Therese was the oldest. They were a very poor family. The fact that they had ten children didn't help their economic situation. There was a blessing to this, however. They were able to appreciate the free gifts of the Lord. They were never prisoners of material possessions. There is a freedom to this that many of us, especially in the United States, can never know. Therese's soul was able to soar to great heights, not being weighed down by things of the world.

She had a desire to join the Missionary Sisters of St. Benedict, in order to work in the Missions in Africa. She planned this from an early age. She was waiting for her younger brothers and sisters to grow up, so that she would not be needed at home. As a young girl, although she was very spiritual, she was not above helping out at home. Her father was drafted into the service during the First World War. The whole family had to band together to make ends meet in this time of his absence.

She was hired out to work on a farm. This helped support her, and bring a meager amount of money into the family. An accident befell Therese while she was helping to put out a fire in a barn. Her spine was permanently damaged. The pain was so great that she lost her balance, and was subject to painful falls. Eventually, she was confined to her bed, an invalid. To make matters worse, the following year she went blind. There is no reason given for this. For the next four years, however, she was totally blind.

Before her father had gone off to war, he had given Therese a little prayer card of St. Therese of Lisieux. She prayed the prayer on the card daily, to the point of memorizing it. After she had become blind, she continued to say this prayer. On April 29, 1923, she said the prayer to her mentor, St. Therese. She fell into a half sleep. She dreamt that someone was touching her pillow. When she awoke, to her amazement, she could see.

She continued suffering severe pains from her back injury. Her lameness continued. The muscles of her left leg contracted, pulling the leg up to the thigh. Having to remain on her back, in this extremely uncomfortable position, she suffered bed sores on her back and legs. Her ankle was badly infected for close to six months, so badly that the bone was exposed. At one point, she put a rose petal which had touched the body of St. Therese of Lisieux on her ankle. Miraculously, the ankle was healed. The skin covered over the bone.

Therese experienced complete healing in her leg and her back on May 17, 1925. Therese experienced a great pain in her back. She screamed, causing her parents to run quickly up the stairs to her room. She was staring blankly into space. Abruptly, she sat up. This was impossible. Her mother lifted the blanket. Her gnarled left leg had straightened out completely. Therese still seemed to be in a trance. She told them, "I can sit up now and even walk." She stared into space, her eyes riveted on some unseen object. When asked what she was looking at, she wouldn't share her experience with anyone. Finally, her confessor asked everyone to leave the room.

When they were alone, her confessor asked her where she'd been. She said that she had seen a bright light, and then heard a voice, asking her if she wanted to be healed. Therese had answered that she was submissive to God's will. She said "I want anything and everything that comes from God. I am happy with all the flowers and birds, or with any other suffering He sends. And what I like most of all is our Dear Savior Himself."

The voice said to her "Today you may have another little joy. You can sit up; try it once. I'll help you." She was lifted up by her right hand, and felt an excruciating pain in her vertebrae, followed by a cracking sound and feeling. After this, the pain was gone. The voice continued speaking to her. "You can walk, too, but you still have very much and very long to suffer and no doctor can help you either. Only through suffering can you best work out your desire and your vocation to be a victim, and thereby help the work of the priests. Through suffering you will gain more souls than through the most brilliant sermons."

We stop now to point out two important phrases in the story above: *May 17, 1925* and *I'll help you.* The voice that came to the aid of Therese didn't identify himself/herself. There is no way for sure to determine who it was. All that Therese saw was a bright light. However, we do know that she had a fervent devotion to, and prayed constantly for, the intervention of St. Therese of Lisieux, the Little Flower. As it happens, the day that her total healing came about was May 17, 1925, the date of the canonization of St. Therese of Lisieux.

Assuming that it was the Little Flower of Lisieux who had visited her namesake, Therese Neumann, she summed up what was to be the life's work, the vocation of this young girl. She was to be a victim. This prophecy was to materialize in the form of the Stigmata, the physical wounds of the Crucified Christ, beginning on March 4, 1926, when blood gushed from her heart, after she had a vision of Jesus suffering the agony in the Garden. The wounds of the Lord continued through that Lent, so that before Easter, she had the five wounds of Jesus in her hands, her feet, and her side. These remained with her for the rest of her life.

It is very difficult to give a thumbnail sketch of the life of this woman. She is such an intriguing Suffering Servant of Christ, and had so many charisms, that we would like to go on in great detail about them all. However, we have to go back to the main reason for bringing Therese Neumann into this book at all, and that is her connection with the Eucharist.

From the time of her first illness, Therese had difficulty taking food into her system. From Christmas of 1922 onwards, she could only take liquid nourishment. But in August of 1926, she experienced a strong aversion to any form of food. Christmas of 1926 was the last time she took any nourishment, other than the Eucharist and some water. In September 1927, she refused even the water. It's reported that this woman lived on nothing but the Body and Blood of Christ for 35 years, until the end of her life in 1962.

Possibly because she lived in our time, there are many eye-witness and sworn statements attesting to the fact that she did not eat, nor experience hunger or thirst. There are reports that she would work in the fields or in the garden of her home for hours, while other people were present, and never take any food or drink. People who had her staying at their homes for days at a time testified that she took nothing at all, except the Blessed Sacrament.

She was asked to undergo medical observations to verify that she took no food. The bishop of the area determined how long a human could live without food. It was suggested that she be tested for eleven days. The bishop settled on fifteen days. Therese was under 24-hour-a-day surveillance. There were al-ways at least two of a four-person nursing team with her. They measured everything that went in or out of her body, including water to rinse her mouth, and her excretions.

The report made at the end of the testing period verified that she had taken no food or drink for the fifteen days. Her weight at the beginning of the testing was the same as at the end, 121 pounds. The only variation on this occurred every Fri-day. On that day each week, she suffered the Passion of Christ. Her weight dropped to 112 1/2 pounds on one Friday, and 115 on another. But by midweek both times, her weight had climbed back to 121.

When asked what she lived on, her constant reply was "On our Savior", which meant the Eucharist.

There are other important things regarding Therese Neu-mann and the Eucharist which we'd like to bring out. She had a strong sensitivity to the Eucharist. She always knew when she was in the presence of Our Lord Jesus in the Eucharist, even when priests were not. There are many reports regarding this. One time she was with Fr. Naber, her confessor. They entered

the church, which was undergoing repairs. At the altar of the
Blessed Sacrament, the altar lamp was out, so everybody assumed that the Lord had been taken out of the Tabernacle
during construction. Therese stopped everyone from walking
past the altar, admonishing them to kneel in the presence of the
Lord. The priest assured her that the Lord was not in the
Tabernacle, but Therese insisted. When the associate pastor
came out of the Sacristy, he told them that the Lord had been
put back into the Tabernacle because the repairs were completed. The Altar Lamp was not lit because they had run out of
oil.

Another unusual report took place in 1932. Therese and Fr.
Naber entered the rectory on a Sunday after Mass. Therese immediately sensed the presence of our Lord in the Eucharist in
the room. The priest told her it was impossible, but Therese
would not relent. She began walking around the room until she
came upon a pile of mail. She ruffled through the envelopes,
picking one out of the middle. She picked it up and handed it to
the priest. "He's in here." she said. The priest opened the enve-
lope. There, between the folds of a white piece of paper, was a
Consecrated Host.

It has been said that Therese Neumann, on occasions when
she went into ecstasy prior to receiving Communion, did not actually swallow the Host. The priest put it on her tongue. She
moved her tongue inward slightly, but never closed her mouth
or swallowed. The Host disappeared. The author of her first
biography, Fritz Gerlich, wrote that the pastor of the parish
church, Fr. Naber, called him in to witness the event himself.
He wrote exactly what he had experienced.

"The Communion took place in the following manner.
When the priest with the ciborium came to the corner of the altar, Therese Neumann, upon looking at the Host, would fall into
ecstasy and show an intense desire to go up to meet our Savior,
but her chair prevented her from rising because its arms closed
in the front. Her face beamed, her eyes shone, her hands were

stretched forward, her feet were in motion. Her whole body rose somewhat off the chair, as if she wanted to get up. The priest gave me a sign to kneel down directly in front of him, so that I could look straight into her open mouth. I did. When the host came near, she opened her mouth wide and put out her tongue. She held her hands over her breast. The priest laid a whole host on the front of her tongue and then left. She drew in her tongue a little, with the host still visible on it, but only far enough so that the tip of her tongue still touched her lower lip and only covered the teeth of her lower jaw, so that I could still see the back part of her tongue and gums.

Suddenly the host disappeared. Her mouth stayed open for a short time. From the time she first opened her mouth, she never closed it, nor did she make any attempt to swallow. Nor could the host be seen in her oral cavity and gums—they had remained open the whole time. After some time of deep interior concentration, she began a long ecstatic conversation. During the whole time that followed, there were no swallowing motions to be noted. No water was offered to her. I must note that the priest had already contacted me on Friday evening, telling me, after he had listened to Therese Neumann's explanation in her ecstatic state, that I should come and witness her reception of Holy Communion, in order to see the new phenomena. Thus on Saturday morning, I was well aware of what I was supposed to pay particular attention to. The spot in the Church was very bright."

Therese Neumann was known to have received Our Lord in the Eucharist by means of what we may call telecommunion, without the assistance of the priest. When she received her First Holy Communion, children were not allowed to receive Communion often. In school, they were taught and encouraged to practise Spiritual Communion. Therese testified in later years that a number of times in her life, while praying in front of the tabernacle at Church for Our Lord to come to her, she actually saw the Host float from the Tabernacle to her. She received

Communion directly from Our Lord Jesus.

It is also reported that when Therese received Communion, the Host did not dissolve in her stomach until just before she was to receive Communion again. She told her Spiritual Director about this many times, but there was never any way to verify the feeling that she had. On one occasion however, long after she had received Communion, Therese became violently ill. She threw up. The Host came out of her mouth, completely intact, many hours after she had received It. It was kept on a clean handkerchief. Therese cried bitterly that Our Lord had been taken away from her. After a time, the Host disappeared. Therese went into a state of ecstasy which always followed her reception of Communion. The Host had gone back inside her body.

There are probably many other saints and holy people who have lived solely on the Eucharist for various periods of time. We've chosen these special people to write about because the circumstances were extraordinary. In these instances, the people of God, His friends, put themselves completely in His hands for their physical as well as spiritual nourishment. Had He chosen not to act on their behalf, they would have died. But we believe that there's more involved here than Our Lord coming to the aid of these people. We believe that there's a strong lesson for us to learn from these miraculous experiences. We believe that the Lord is our nourishment. He told us so. But that was a long time ago. Many of us have lost our faith in this promise. As in the Eucharistic Miracles, Jesus uses these people and these miracles to prove to us that He is with us, and that He feeds us with His Body and Blood.

We thank you Jesus. We praise Your Holy Name. We ask You to continue to feed us, even when we don't believe that we're being fed. But most of all, Jesus, help us to believe.

Epilogue

There are 130 reported Eucharistic Miracles such as the ones we have just studied. Many are local folklore, which have no documentation to support the stories. Others are called "Doubtful Miracles", because of some shadow of doubt cast over the event, or the substantiation. We chose to write on the miracles that are in this book because: (1)There is solid substantiation by the Church, after intensive investigation, to back up the miracles; (2)In most instances, the miracle is still at the shrine for us to venerate, or a shrine has been erected, telling the story as in the miracles of Turin and Erding; (3)There is still a strong devotion to Our Lord Jesus in the Eucharist, as presented to the faithful in the particular miracle at these shrines; (4)We have visited most of these shrines ourselves, and so we have first-hand knowledge of them.

We have come a long way together, sharing the special Gifts the Lord has given us through these miracles. Our eleven years of research were spread out. We visited different shrines at different times. We would visit a shrine; then we wrote on that shrine. It was all done at different times. Even the slide presentations we made were only about a few of the miracles. But spending eight months writing on them, putting everything together into one book, has been overwhelming.

There are more Eucharistic Miracles than we've written about. It would take another three years to research all of them. We're just not sure we have another three years. We have had a great urgency to get this book out immediately. We're not even sure why. We truly believe the Lord is insisting that we emphasize forcefully the importance of the Miracle of the Eucharist, which has been taken for granted, or put aside as so much Catholic Hocus Pocus. He wants it done *now*.

The number and scope of the Eucharistic Miracles is not really the issue here. If there were only one, if that first Eucharistic Miracle, which took place on Holy Thursday were the only one, *it is enough!* Jesus is trying to get a message across to us, and He's not beyond hitting us over the head with a two-by-four to do it. We've got to begin listening, and taking Him seriously. Time is getting short.

There are just a few things we'd like to point out. We talked about God being a pilot in a plane, way up in the sky, with an infinite visibility. Many of these Eucharistic Miracles seemed at first to be unrelated to events that were happening, or were to happen at some time in the future. But as we looked at the time sequence of events in our world history, or our Church history, a giant jigsaw puzzle started to come together. The pieces began to fit. We could see the reasoning for many of the Eucharistic Miracles, other than the obvious. Just as an example, two seemingly unrelated Eucharistic Miracles, one in Langenwiese, Poland and the other in Turin, Italy at about the same time, had to do with an Arab invasion of Europe that had taken place in Constantinople, hundreds of miles away from either place.

The most obvious sequence of events was that involved in God's Plan for the institution of the Feast in honor of the Blessed Sacrament, manifested in the Eucharistic Miracle of Bolsena, Italy. He took a period of 70 years, and people from all over the continent of Europe, to create a miracle, which was the thrust He used to have this Feast Day instituted. As if this miracle were not enough to convince Pope Urban IV, He had a group from Daroca, Spain come to Rome to tell the Pope about the Eucharistic Miracle that had occurred there. When the Lord decides to make something happen, it happens. He will have His way.

For us, the greatest emotion to come out of all of this was excitement. Our Faith is exciting, and Our Lord Jesus is powerful. Possibly more than anything else is the fact that He is always there with us. He proves that He watches over everything that happens to us. We don't have to be afraid that we're all alone. How many times have we felt abandoned, without hope? But it's not necessary! He's there always. All we have to do is reach out and call Him. Our life can be joyful in the Lord. It's easy. All you have to do is say "yes".

Bibliography

Atlante Mondiale - Instituto Geografico - Novara, Italy 1974

Bargellini, Piero *The Little Flowers of St. Clare* - Messagero
Editions Milan, Italy 1972

Bargellini, Piero *Mille Santi dei Giorno* - Valecchi, Italy 1978

Butler, Thurston, Atwater - *Lives of the Saints*
Christian Classics - Westminster, Md 1980

Centi, Fr. Tino S. O.P. *Il Tesoro Eucaristico de Siena* 1979

Chabas, Roque - *Los Corporales de Daroca* - Valencia, 1905

Haesle, M. *Eucharistische Wunder aus aller Welt* Zurich 1968

Johnston, Francis - *Alexandrina* Veritas Pub. Dublin 1979

Ladame Jean & Duvin Richard *Prodiges Eucharistiques*
Editions France Empire - Paris - 1981

Laurentin, Rene *A Hundred Years Ago Bernadette*
Fetes & Saisons, Editions du Cerf, Paris 1979

Le Saint Sang de Miracle a Bois-Seigneur-Isaac 1961

Mosconi, Antonio *Guida Storico di Bagno di Romagno* 1978

New American Bible Thomas A. Nelson Co. New York 1970

Omnibus of St. Francis of Assisi Franciscan Herald Press 1972

Piccini Ugo *Il Tesoro Eucarstico di Siena*, 1978

Puri, Msgr - *Bolsena, Breve Guida* Edizioni Torre, 1982

Sammaciccia, Bruno, *Eucharistic Miracle of Lanciano* 1976

Steiner, Johannes Therese Neumann Alba House, N.Y. 1967

Journeys of Faith®   **www.bobandpennylord.com**
To Order: 1-800-633-2484   email info@bobandpennylord.com
Bob and Penny Lord are authors of these best selling books:
This Is My Body, This Is My Blood;
Miracles of the Eucharist Book I Paperback
This Is My Body, This Is My Blood;
Miracles of the Eucharist Book II Paperback
The Many Faces Of Mary, A Love Story Paperback Hardcover
Saints and Other Powerful Women in the Church Paperback
Saints and Other Powerful Men in the Church Paperback
Heavenly Army of Angels Paperback
Scandal of the Cross and Its Triumph Paperback
The Rosary - The Life of Jesus and Mary Hardcover
Martyrs - They Died for Christ Paperback
Visionaries, Mystics, and Stigmatists Paperback
Visions of Heaven, Hell and Purgatory Paperback
Treasures of the Church - That which makes us Catholic Paperback
Tragedy of the Reformation Paperback
Cults - Battle of the Angels 5 Paperback
Church Trilogy (3 Books - Treasures..., Tragedy... and Cults...) Paperback
Journey to Sainthood - Founders, Confessors & Visionaries Paperback
Holy Innocence - The Young and the Saintly Paperback
Defenders of the Faith - Saints of the Counter-Reformation Paperback
Super Saints Trilogy (3 Books - Journey ... Holy... Defenders...)
Beyond Sodom and Gomorrah Paperback
The Journey and the Dream, Our Love Story Paperback
Miracles of the Cross Paperback
Miracles of the Child Jesus Paperback
The Many Faces of Mary Book II Paperback
Saints, Maligned, Misunderstood & Mistreated Paperback
Please add $5.00 S&H for first book: $1.00 each add'l book

Videos and On-site Documentaries
Video Series based on Bob and Penny's books:13 part series on the Miracles of the Eucharist - 15 part series on The Many Faces of Mary - 23 part series on Martyrs - They Died for Christ - 10 part series on Visionaries, Mystics and Stigmatists - 50 part series on the Super Saints Trilogy - 17 part series on Scandal of the Cross and Its Triumph. Many other on-site Documentaries based on Miracles of the Eucharist, Mother Mary's Apparitions, and the Angels. Books and videos available in Spanish also.

Pilgrimages
Bob and Penny Lord's ministry take out Pilgrimages to the Shrines of Europe, and Canada every year. Come and join them on one of these special Retreat Pilgrimages. Call for more information, and ask for the latest pilgrimage brochure. Call 1-888-262-5673.

Lecture Series
Bob and Penny travel to all parts of the world to spread the Good News. They speak on what they have written about in their books. If you would like to have them come to your area, call 1-800-633-2484 for information on a lecture series in your area.

Good Newsletter
We are publishers of the Good Newsletter, which is published four times a year. This newsletter will provide timely articles on our Faith, plus keep you informed with the activities of our community. Call 1-800-633-2484 for information.